What readers are saying about
Agile Retrospectives

Esther Derby and Diana Larsen have written the definitive book on agile retrospectives. You don't have to be an agile team to take advantage of their book; you only have to want to improve. Follow their advice and your teams will be more successful.

➤ **Johanna Rothman**
   Author, speaker and consultant, Rothman Consulting Group, Inc.

Two of the software industry's leading facilitators have taken their many years of retrospective experience and distilled them into an approachable reference for agile team leaders. For all of the self-made facilitators out there who have been winging it, this book will provide a solid foundation to improve the effectiveness of your iteration, release, and project retrospectives.

➤ **Dave Hoover**
   Lead Consultant, Agile Practices, Obtiva Corp.

This book is a wonderful compendium of ways to keep retrospectives fresh and teams learning.

➤ **Mike Cohn**
    Author of *Agile Estimating and Planning*

This book is a must-read for all team leads, facilitators and everyone interested in driving improvements in the ways teams reflect, learn and function.

➤ **Sheila O'Connor, Ph.D.**
    Six Sigma Software Black Belt, LSI Logic, Engenio Storage Group

Whatever you call it: retrospective, post-mortem, post-partum, post-project review. Your work can be better by stopping at regular intervals and asking, "What worked well that we don't want to forget? What should be done differently?" It's almost like free consulting with two of the best: Esther Derby and Diana Larsen. I facilitate retrospectives for a living and, believe me, I'm going to read my copy cover to cover—more than once!

➤ **Linda Rising**
    Co-author of *Fearless Change: Patterns for Introducing New Ideas*

Agile Retrospectives

Making Good Teams Great

Esther Derby

Diana Larsen

The Pragmatic Bookshelf

Dallas, Texas • Raleigh, North Carolina

Many of the designations used by manufacturers and sellers to distinguish their products are claimed as trademarks. Where those designations appear in this book, and The Pragmatic Programmers, LLC was aware of a trademark claim, the designations have been printed in initial capital letters or in all capitals. The Pragmatic Starter Kit, The Pragmatic Programmer, Pragmatic Programming, Pragmatic Bookshelf, PragProg and the linking *g* device are trademarks of The Pragmatic Programmers, LLC.

Every precaution was taken in the preparation of this book. However, the publisher assumes no responsibility for errors or omissions, or for damages that may result from the use of information (including program listings) contained herein.

Our Pragmatic courses, workshops, and other products can help you and your team create better software and have more fun. For more information, as well as the latest Pragmatic titles, please visit us at *http://pragprog.com*.

Printed in the United States of America.
ISBN-13: 978-0-9776-1664-0
Printed on acid-free paper.
Book version: P7.0—August 2012

Contents

Foreword

On my birthdays, I look back and reflect on my life. How have things gone? Where did I think I would be thirty years ago, ten years ago, one year ago? Where am I now? How could I do things better, and what things that I rue should I just resolve so I can get past them? Am I the type of person I hoped to be, and is the impact I have on others what I would hope for? If not, what might I do differently in the upcoming year(s)? Have I used the strength and intelligence that I have wisely?

This is my retrospective. I look back and assess. I consider. Taking everything into account, I try to set a better course for the upcoming year. I'm really glad that nobody is keeping score, even me, because I don't know how well I'm doing overall. I guess it depends on philosophies that keep changing and on circumstances that bring more variability than I ever expected. Who could have predicted what my children would be like?

Maybe if I had clearer goals and more frequent birthdays, the retrospectives would work better. I'll bet that if I had Esther and Diana at my more frequent birthdays, things would work out better. An outside facilitator with techniques like they spell out in this book would provide new insights and help formulate more concrete next steps.

I've been using iterative, incremental (a.k.a. Agile)) processes formally for eleven years; my drink of choice is called Scrum. The goals are very clear in Scrum. They are established for a project and then reset for every iteration. Since these iterations are every thirty days, there isn't a lot of wandering. Since the domain is building software, not just life in general, it is also easier to tell whether progress is in the right direction or needs adjusting. Because Scrum is a team activity, the group reflection is particularly helpful. Everyone chips in, and the surprises are manifold.

Edward Yourdon described the long, terrible progress through a project in *Death March* (Prentice Hall, 1997). A problem with these projects is that there are no birthdays and no regular points for reflection and readjustment.

The natural rhythm of the iterative delivery of software in Agile projects provides such a break point. These are chances for the team to improve what it is doing and how they feel about what they are doing. What an opportunity. Read Esther and Diana's book and see how it works.

➤ **Ken Schwaber**
  Scrum Author and Evangelist
  Scrum Alliance

Preface

When we say *retrospective*, here's what we have in mind: a special meeting where the team gathers after completing an increment of work to inspect and adapt their methods and teamwork. Retrospectives enable whole-team learning, act as catalysts for change, and generate action. Retrospectives go beyond checklist project audits or perfunctory project closeouts. And, in contrast to traditional postmortems or project reviews, retrospectives focus not only on the development process, but on the team and team issues. And team issues are as challenging as technical issues—if not more so.

We have been leading retrospectives and teaching others to lead retrospectives for a combined twenty years. In fact, in 2003, we were bestowed with the title Retrospective Goddesses at the annual Retrospective Facilitators Gathering in Baden, Austria. It's not every day you get to read a book written by a pair of goddesses! Although we don't really claim divinity, we do know lots about helping teams learn together in retrospectives.

We've talked to people who claim that retrospectives are a waste of time. When we probe for details, the process they describe doesn't resemble what we would call a retrospective. However, when people follow a process similar to what we describe in this book, we've seen solid, bottom-line results.

Our clients and colleagues tell us that they see benefits from retrospectives, too. Here's some of what we've seen and heard. In each case the team identified improvements during their retrospective and applied new practices in the next iteration.

Improved Productivity   A team in California reduced rework at the end of their next release by improving their unit testing. They added more tests and tested more frequently. Because they were finding errors earlier, they didn't have to scramble at the end of the release.

Improved Capability   A team in Florida used their retrospective to devise a solution to a long-standing problem. Only one person on the team knew how to integrate client data with the corporate database. The team set up a pairing schedule that enabled other team members to learn about the database and eliminated the bottleneck.

Improved Quality   A team in Minnesota observed a clear connection between lack of customer contact during their iterations and missed requirements. They increased customer involvement during subsequent iterations to reduce misunderstandings and rework on features. As collaboration with the customer increased, the team spent less time re-hashing and more time preventing defects and refactoring.

Increased Capacity   A team in New York examined how they prioritized features and moved from yearly to quarterly releases by focusing on delivering smaller high-value feature sets.

Along with bottom line benefits, retrospectives have a way of increasing empowerment and enjoyment for teams.

After performing iteration retrospectives for a year, a team in London reported that retrospectives had changed their lives for the better. Another team called in a social worker when they faced an especially tough problem. After observing the team, the social worker pointed out that the team had better skills for navigating conflict than most of the professional social workers he knew (*XP—Call in the Social Workers* [Mac03]). The team knew how to have the uncomfortable—but necessary—conversations to resolve disagreements before they escalated into conflict or resentment.

We can't predict the results you'll achieve, but the evidence shows that retrospectives can improve teamwork, methods, work satisfaction, and results.

We want to thank our reviewers for their invaluable help. This book wouldn't be what it is without them: Tim Bacon, Raj Balasubramanian, Nicole Belilos, Johannes Brodwall, Brandon Campbell, Mike Cohn, Rachel Davies, Dale Emery, Marc Evers, Pat Eyler, Caton Gates, David Greenfield, Daniel Grenner, Elisabeth Hendrickson, Darcy Hitchcock, Dave Hoover, Stephen Jenkins, Bil Kleb, Willem Larsen, Anthony Lauder, Sunil Menda, Sheila O'Connor, David Pickett, Wes Reisz, Linda Rising, Johanna Rothman, Matt Secoske, Guerry Semones, Dave W. Smith, Michael Stok, and Bas Vodde.

We would be remiss if we didn't thank Norm Kerth. Norm is the elder statesman of retrospectives and has worked to make retrospectives common practice. We've both known Norm for years, and in fact, he's the one who introduced us to each other. We found common ground with Norm in work that each of us was doing independently and, out of that common ground, started the Retrospective Facilitators Gathering in 2001.

We want to thank the members of the Retrospective Facilitators Gathering. Each year we meet with people who are doing amazing work with retrospectives. At the first gathering in Oregon, four countries were represented (Austria, Denmark, the Netherlands and the USA). The 2006 gathering, held in Germany, brought together people from eleven countries. The people of the gathering are generous with their insights, experiences, and activities.

Finally, we want to thank Andy Hunt, Dave Thomas, and Steve Peter at the Pragmatic Bookshelf. We couldn't have done it without you.

Introduction

Suppose you are a member of a software development team. You're doing good work, but not great work. You're starting to see signs of interpersonal friction on the team, and some people you would like to retain on the team are dusting off their résumés. You know you need to adapt your practices and ease the interpersonal tension before things get worse. You want to introduce retrospectives to your team.

Maybe you are a team lead, and you've heard about retrospectives but have never tried one. You've heard retrospectives can help teams perform better, but you're not sure where to start.

Maybe you've been holding retrospectives for months, and your team isn't coming up with any new ideas. You need a way revitalize your retrospectives so the team doesn't lose the gains they've made.

Whatever the reason you've picked up this book, we assume you think retrospectives might help your team. Whether you're a coach, a team member, or a project manager and whether you're expected to lead retrospectives after every iteration or are initiating retrospectives for the first time, you'll find ideas and techniques that you can apply to your situation.

Our main focus in this book is short retrospectives—retrospectives that occur after one week to one month of work. Whether you are using Agile methods or more traditional incremental or iterative development, your team has an opportunity to reflect at the end of every increment and identify changes and improvements that will increase the quality of the product and the work life of team members.

Retrospectives are a natural fit in an Agile work environment—Scrum and Crystal explicitly include "inspect and adapt" cycles for the methods and teamwork along with mechanisms to examine and improve the product. While continuous builds, automated unit tests, and frequent demonstrations of working code are all ways to focus attention on the product and allow the team to make adjustments, retrospectives focus attention on how the team does their work and interacts.

Retrospectives are also a natural fit in a team environment—where there are less than ten in the team and the work is interdependent. Retrospectives help people improve practices, handle issues, and surface obstacles on a regular basis.

Iteration retrospectives focus on real problems that affect teams. During retrospectives, teams discover real solutions that they can implement without waiting for management's permission. Since experiments and changes are chosen, not imposed from above, people are more invested in their success.

When we started leading retrospectives more than a decade ago, most retrospectives looked at whole projects that had run for a year or more. In the past ten years, there has been a shift. More and more teams are working in shorter iterations and releasing software more frequently. These teams no longer wait until the end of a long project to inspect and adapt. They look for ways to improve at the end of every iteration. Team coaches, team leads, and team members now lead their own retrospectives.

Even if your team isn't using Agile methods, you can adapt the advice in this book to inspect and adapt your processes and teamwork before the end of a project: hold a retrospective every month or so or at project milestones.

You may need to convince your managers that this is a good use of your time and company dollars. A growing body of financial and empirical data shows that consistent retrospectives result in real savings and improvements.

In this book, we'll introduce a structure for retrospectives and walk through the process of planning, designing, and leading a retrospective. We'll supply activities and guidance on how to use them, and we'll share stories from real retrospectives.

We've also included a chapter on the role of the retrospective leader. We believe that most people can lead retrospectives with confidence and competence—and help the team achieve results—with a good structure and the right tools.

And, we've included examples of how you can adjust the basic retrospective structure for a three-month release or a yearlong project—and anything in between. Even if the team disbands after the release or project, the organization can learn from a retrospective, and individuals will take the learning with them.

CHAPTER 1

Helping Your Team Inspect and Adapt

Retrospectives help teams—even great ones—keep improving. In this chapter, we'll start with an example of an hour-long iteration retrospective. We'll watch what the retrospective leader does, and then we'll analyze the example so you can apply the process to your retrospectives.

Let's peek in on a team who writes financial software as they hold their retrospective at the end of a two-week iteration. This team rotates leadership of the retrospective, and this week, it's Dana's turn to lead.

After all the team members are seated in a semicircle facing a large white board with several posters at one end, Dana starts the retrospective.

"Here we are again, taking time to examine our work in the last iteration. We have an hour blocked to focus on our teamwork and methods. It's 4 PM now; we should be finished by 5. This time, we're going to focus on our development processes, because we've noticed that the number of defects is increasing."

"Before we look at the data, let's do a quick check-in: in a word or two, what's going on for you as we start this retrospective?"

Each of the six team members gave a short response. "I'm puzzled," said the first.

"Curious," said the second.

"Bummed about the defects," answered the third.

"Hey, that's more than a word or two!" said the first team member and gave the wordy team member a poke in the arm.

"OK. Bummed," he corrected.

The last two gave their responses, and Dana moved on.

"Do we need any amendments to our usual working agreements for this meeting?" Dana asked, gesturing to the working agreements posted on the wall. After all agreed the working agreements were sufficient, Dana outlined the process for the meeting.

"First we'll look at our data and then brainstorm and cluster possible causes. After that, we'll generate some ideas to approach the problem in our next iteration, choose one, and design an experiment. Sound OK?"

When all agreed, Dana moved to the next step.

"Let's look at our defect data," Dana said, pointing to a large chart that showed each feature they'd worked on and the number of defects they'd found in their own testing. "What was going on here?" she asked. "Give me a read on what was going on as you worked on each of these features." She handed out small, colored sticky notes. "Let's look at what was going on during the iteration—post the events you remember. Then put an orange sticky note where there was frustration."

"Hmm," a team member mused as she put the last orange sticky note on the wall. "I'm surprised that the frustration isn't clustered with the defects. I wonder what that's about."

"Let's see whether we can answer that. Take five minutes to write down everything we know and then see what patterns we can discern." Dana handed out larger sticky notes and markers.

One team member wrote furiously. Another stared at the chart for a minute and then started jotting down notes. Two others talked quietly and compared ideas as they started writing.

At the end of five minutes, team members walked to the white board and stuck their sticky notes on it.

"Which of these seem like they might have a similar cause?" Dana asked. Team members moved the sticky notes around, putting two or three close together and then moving them apart as they talked about what was written on each sticky note.

At the end of ten minutes, there were four distinct clusters, which the team labeled as follows: inconsistent pairing, too rushed to do test-driven development, code smells, and legacy code.

"What do you see here?" Dana asked, starting a discussion of the contributing factors.

"Which one of these causes is causing most of the defects?" Dana asked.

The answer was unanimous: legacy code. "Let's take a minute to brainstorm experiments we can do in the next iteration to bring the defect rates down."

The team quickly identified five different approaches.

"Dot vote," Dana commanded. "Two dots per person; use them any way you want."

In two minutes they had a top choice.

"Now let's design our experiment," Dana prompted.

The team worked for fifteen minutes identifying the action steps required for the experiment:

- Schedule a walk-through with Sally from the Support group (she worked with this code for years).
- Write unit tests for the area of legacy code we're touching.
- Enlist Sally to pair with us one or two mornings a week.

Dana looked at her watch. They had five minutes left. "What about the pairing? We agreed we'd pair four hours a day."

"That's right, Dana," a team member responded. "We need to do better on that. I'll put up a pairing dashboard so we remind ourselves."

"OK, time to wrap up. How will we know we're succeeding with our legacy code experiment?" Dana asked.

"We'll see fewer defects in this area of the code base," one team member offered, and the others agreed. "Yep, that's the acid test."

"We'll check that at our next retrospective," Dana said. "Whose turn is it to lead next time?" A hand went up. "You'll bring the new data, right?"

"Thanks for your hard work," Dana said. "We'll take these action steps into our planning meeting—which is tomorrow morning at 9 AM."

Let's review what Dana did in this retrospective.

Dana let the group know the purpose, focus, and time allowed for the retrospective. She told them how they would spend their time. She used a brief check-in to allow everyone to speak and reviewed the team's already established working agreements.

Dana reviewed the team's defect data and then asked about events and areas of frustration. She did this so everyone was considering the same data, rather than only the data each individual knew about. She asked the team to examine facts—the defect data—and feelings—the areas of frustration.

Dana led the group to interpret the data and discern patterns.

Dana helped the group identify approaches, choose an approach, and plan to achieve a goal related to the focus of the retrospective.

Dana ended the session decisively. She confirmed with the group how they would assess progress, and thanked them for their participation.

Dana followed a specific structure:

1. Set the stage.

2. Gather data.

3. Generate insights.

4. Decide what to do.

5. Close the retrospective.

Every year at the Retrospective Facilitators Gathering, we learn about new ways and new twists on old ways to lead retrospectives. And we return to this structure because it works for us—and it can work for you. This structure can fit into an hour or expand to three days. You can add variety by adding new activities, but stick to this basic outline—this structure does what a retrospective needs to do.

In this chapter, we'll look at each phase in the structure.

1.1 Set the Stage

Setting the stage helps people focus on the work at hand. It reiterates the goal for the time the team has together in the retrospective. And, it contributes to creating an atmosphere where people feel comfortable discussing issues.

Start with a simple welcome and appreciation for people's investment of time. Restate the purpose of the retrospective and the goal for the session. Remind people of how long you'll meet.

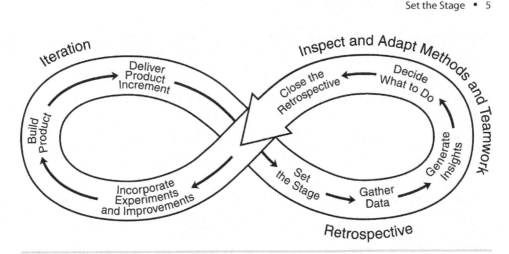

Figure 1—Retrospective steps as part of an iterative life cycle

Then ask everyone in the room to speak. When someone doesn't speak at the beginning of the retrospective, that person has tacit permission to remain silent for the rest of the session. Since the point of the retrospective is to help the group think and learn together, you need everyone's participation. This isn't the time for a long dissertation—or even a short one. (Do the math. If each person on a ten-person team spoke for three minutes, you'd spend thirty minutes just on introductions. Even with a five-person team, the time adds up.) Ask for a word or two describing a hope for the retrospective.

Next, outline the approach for the session. Time is precious, and people want to know that their time will be well spent. Knowing the approach helps establish that this won't be another aimless meeting.

After you've established the timebox, goal, and approach, work to establish an environment where people can bring up difficult topics and have challenging conversations. Team values and working agreements are both types of social contracts that describe acceptable behavior and interactions. We're not talking about abstract, high-falutin' statements such as "We value all people equally" (even though you might). We're talking about working agreements that do real work to help people talk about tough issues, bring up emotional topics, or deliver unwelcome news.

If your team has a set of values, use them. Remind them that their values also hold for the retrospective. The team may need to adapt some values so they fit the retrospective.

Every Voice

At the end of one retrospective, Brenda piped up. "I'm surprised I talked so much."

Others nodded in agreement. "Yeah, Brenda usually keeps quiet. I'm really glad she talked so much this time. She had a lot to say."

"How did you persuade me to talk?" Brenda asked.

The answer was simple: the retrospective leader asked her to say her name within the first five minutes.

This sounds too simple to be true, yet it works.

An XP team had named quality, simplicity, teamwork, and courage as their values. A team member asked how the value of simplicity applied to a retrospective. Their coach suggested that simplicity might mean finding the simplest improvement actions that could possibly work. Others supplied ideas on what quality, teamwork, and courage would look like in the retrospective.

Likewise, if your team has working agreements, post them and review them. Adjust the working agreements as needed to apply in the retrospective.

A game development team's first working agreement was "The job of every programming pair is to make sure the code is ready for the next pair." For the retrospective, the team reinterpreted this as "The job of every subteam is to have their work ready for the entire retrospective group."

If your team doesn't have working agreements, develop them now—before proceeding. It's impossible to anticipate every situation; most groups can address the majority of situations with five working agreements. If you need more than the fingers on both hands to count your working agreements, you have too many.

Here's an example of why you need working agreements at the start of the retrospective: Fran's cell phone starts ringing just as the group broaches a sensitive topic. At this point, it's awkward to say, "Don't answer that phone!" And it feels capricious to people when they learn what the rules are only after they've been broken. If your team has a working agreement that says "Mobile phones on silent during meetings," it's less disruptive to point to the agreement and end the interruption. It also feels more fair to the people in the retrospective. The last thing you want is to look like a petty tyrant when you are leading a retrospective.

You get another benefit: working agreements make everyone responsible for civil behavior and collaboration, not just the retrospective leader (*Helping Your Team Weather the Storm* [Der05]).

The first time your team develops working agreements in a retrospective, they might spend ten to fifteen minutes on them—but the agreements are reusable in future retrospectives and in daily work.

Tip 1: Working Agreements Belong to the Team

Ask your team to monitor their working agreements during the retrospective. When your team takes responsibility for their interactions, you can focus on facilitating.

As the team develops or adjusts their working agreements, notice what comes up. Working agreements are often a clue to what people are worried about.

Here's a story: as Chris, a tech lead from outside the team, helped establish working agreements with a team who wrote chemical analysis software, the group identified "Everyone participates" as a working agreement.

As they started the first activity, Chris realized that the group had been worried about Dave, their "star" performer. In the first group discussion, Dave went on and on giving his perspective. When other team members attempted to join the conversation, Dave dismissed them with a wave and kept talking. Chris supported the team in holding their agreement by recording Dave's comments and saying "Thank you, Dave; now let's hear from someone else." After that, team members were more assertive with Dave. Dave still had a great deal to say, but he didn't dominate the discussion.

The first welcome through reviewing working agreements can take as little as five minutes. Inexperienced retrospective leaders like to skip setting the stage and plow ahead into the "meat" of a retrospective. We never regret spending time setting the stage—and neither should you. "Saving" time by skipping this part costs time later. When people don't speak early, they may not contribute at all—and may not buy into the team's insights and decisions. When they don't know the approach, people have trouble focusing and may take the group on a tangent. Team values and working agreements help keep the conversations and interactions productive.

So, don't skip setting the stage, and don't skimp on it either.

1.2 Gather Data

It may seem silly to gather data for an iteration that lasted a week or two. But when someone misses one day in a weeklong iteration, they've missed 20% of the events and interactions. Even when people are present, they don't see everything, and different people have different perspectives on the same event. Gathering data creates a shared picture of what happened. Without a common picture, individuals tend to verify their own opinions and beliefs. Gathering data expands everyone's perspective.

Start with the hard data: events, metrics, features or stories completed, and so forth. Events can include meetings, decision points, changes in team membership, milestones, celebrations, adopting new technologies—any event that had meaning to someone on the team. Metrics include burndown charts, velocity, defect counts, number of stories completed, amount of code refactored, effort data, and so forth. Encourage people to refer to team calendars and other artifacts—documents, emails, charts—to add to the picture.

For an hour-long retrospective, you can ask people to report verbally on data and events or use the team's task board and big visible charts. When your team looks back more than a week or two, create a visual record using a timeline or data charts. A visual depiction of data and events makes it easier for people to see patterns and make connections.

Hard facts are only part of the data. Feelings are at least half the story. Feelings tell what's important to people about the facts and about the team.

Here's a story about a time when looking at feelings helped a team understand the consequence of keeping their concerns to themselves: Pat's team created a timeline by posting cards to represent what happened during their thirty-day iteration. They put green dots on events that were high points and blue dots on low points. When all the dots were in place, one card stood out as shown in Figure 2, *Carly's Card*, on page 9. The card had nine green dots and one blue dot.

Carly confessed that the card and the blue dot were hers. "I felt like I had hijacked the planning session. I can't believe anybody thought that was good."

"Carly, we knew you were upset, but it wasn't until you spoke up that we were able to fix the problem."

Several team members revealed they had concerns similar to Carly's. But because no one was talking about it, no one could solve the issue. Carly's "outburst" was the key to solving an ongoing problem.

CARLY WENT NUTS! in THE PLANNING MEETING

Carly's event card with nine green dots, indicating this event was a high point, and one blue dot, showing it as a low point.

Figure 2—Carly's Card

Without consciously looking for feelings, this conversation wouldn't have happened.

Creating a structured way for people to talk about feelings makes it more comfortable to raise topics that have an emotional charge. When people avoid emotional content, it doesn't go away; it goes underground and saps energy and motivation. Or the emotion may come out in a flare of anger, and a flame war won't help your retrospective.

Before proceeding to the next phase, do a quick review of the data with the entire team. Ask the team to scan the data you've gathered and comment on patterns, shifts, and surprises.

Thorough data gathering, and including both facts and feelings, leads to better thinking and action in the rest of the retrospective. Without a shared picture, people are working from a narrow set of data—their own. When people look only at their own data, the team is less likely to commit to changes and experiments. Without feelings data, the team may not address the topics that are most important to them.

The *F* Word

OK, we're working with engineers here. They may not want to talk about their feelings. So in retrospectives, we usually don't ask people how they feel.

But we have our ways.

Rather than ask directly how people feel, try asking the question a different way:

When were you excited to come to work? When was coming to work "just a job"? When did you dread coming to work?

What were the high points? What were the low points?

How was it to be on this iteration?

When were you [fill in an emotion word—mad, sad, surprised...]?

Questions like these let people talk about how they experienced the iteration without using the *F* word ("feelings").

1.3 Generate Insights

Now is the time to ask "Why?" and begin thinking about what to do differently. When generating insights, the team considers the data to identify strengths and issues from the previous iteration.

Lead the team to examine the conditions, interactions, and patterns that contributed to their success. Investigate breakdowns and deficiencies. Look for risks and unexpected events or outcomes.

It's easy for people to jump to solutions once problems emerge. First solutions may be correct, but often they're not. The work of this phase is to consider additional possibilities, look at causes and effects, and think about them analytically. It's also a time for the team to think together.

These insights help the team see how to work more effectively—which is the ultimate goal of any retrospective.

Generating insights allows the team to step back, see the big picture, and delve into root causes.

When you skip generating insights, your team may not understand how events, behaviors, and circumstances affect their ability to develop software. Time spent generating insights helps ensure that when your team plans an improvement, it's one that will make a positive difference.

> ## Reusable Skills
>
> The activities and skills teams use to generate insights and analyze the problems in a retrospective apply outside the retrospective, too.
>
> Teams can use these analytical tools to understand technical problems, prioritize stories or requirements, plan a strategy, or drive innovation.
>
> For example, a web development team learned a mind-mapping technique during a retrospective. Later, when they experienced friction with their customer, mind mapping helped the team explore options to approach the problem.

1.4   Decide What to Do

At this point, the team has a list of potential experiments and improvements. Now is the time to pick the top items (usually no more than one or two for an iteration) and plan what to do. Your primary job is to provide structure and guidance for your team to plan experiments and actions.

Sometimes teams come up with long lists of candidate improvements; but too many initiatives can overwhelm your ability to change. Pick one or two experiments for the next iteration. Help your team choose items that they can commit to and that will have a positive effect. If your team is recovering from a change that was stressful, help them choose something less complex this time.

Taking action during the retrospective builds momentum. Mike's team created a new working agreement, "Everyone will pair at least four hours a day," to address inconsistent pair programming. Jan's team redesigned their lab and created new check-in procedures.

One way to plan for experiments and changes is to create story cards or backlog items. This makes it easier to incorporate improvement plans into the work plan for the next iteration. Holding your retrospective right before iteration planning is ideal. Plan a break—even if it's only lunch—between the retrospective and the planning session.

Whether you finish planning in the retrospective or incorporate actions into iteration plans, be sure that people sign up and commit to tasks. Without individual commitment, people assume that "the team" will do the task, and no one does it.

Avoiding the Do-Nothing Retrospective

Teams who identify external groups as the source of their ills and want those people to change end up frustrated. Waiting for other people to change is an exercise in futility. The most powerful place to start change is within the team. Even when your team doesn't have direct control, your team can take action to influence or change their own response.

Change happens in the course of normal work. Teams who believe their retrospectives are a waste of time often keep their improvement plans completely separate from their daily work plans. When the plans are separate, no one finds time to do the "extra" work.

1.5 Close the Retrospective

All good things come to an end, even retrospectives. End the retrospective decisively: don't let people (and their energy) dribble away. Decide how to document the experience and plan for follow-up.

Help your team decide how they'll retain what they've learned from the retrospective. Track new practices with posters or big visible charts. Use a digital camera or hit the Print button on that printing white board to create a visual record. The learnings belong to the team, and team members: not the coach, not the team lead, and not you as the retrospective leader. The team needs to own them.

Close the retrospective with an appreciation for the hard work everyone did both during the iteration and during the retrospective.

Before you end, take a few minutes to perform a retrospective on the retrospective. Look at what went well and what you could do differently in the next retrospective. "Inspect and adapt" applies to retrospectives, too.

Using this structure—Set the Stage, Gather Data, Generate Insights, Decide What to Do and Close the Retrospective—will help your team do the following:

- Understand different points of view.

- Follow a natural order of thinking.

- Take a comprehensive view of the team's current methods and practices.

- Allow the discussion to go where it needs to go, rather than predetermining the outcome.

- Leave the retrospective with concrete action and experiments for the next iteration.

The structure gives you, as the retrospective leader, a tried-and-true process to help your team inspect and adapt. In the next chapter, we'll proceed step-by-step through using this structure to create a retrospective that will work for your team.

CHAPTER 2

A Retrospective Custom-Fit to Your Team

When we first started leading retrospectives, outside facilitators conferred with the project sponsor and project manager to determine the goal and approach for an end-of-project retrospective. But if you're a coach or team lead doing iterative development, you're probably leading your own retrospectives after each iteration. You may even be rotating the role among team members. In any case, if you are planning and leading a retrospective, you'll make a series of decisions about the goal, the logistics, and the flow of the session. But before you make decisions, investigate.

2.1 Learning About the History and Environment

If you're leading retrospectives for your own team, you probably already know the history and context. Even so, take a second look. Check your assumptions about the team's history and morale and about the state of the project.

If you're working with a team other than your own, study their context. Scan the team's work space. Look at the cartoons, white boards, and other artifacts. Notice what artifacts are available and which are missing. Talk to formal and informal team leaders. The information you gather will help you work with the team to choose an appropriate goal. What you observe will give you clues about what questions to ask and what problems the team may be facing.

When you talk to people on the team, find out about topics such as these:

- What did this iteration produce? What was the team aiming for? How did the result meet (or not meet) expectations?

- What is the history of previous project reviews? What happened, and what was the follow-up?

- What's going on elsewhere in the organization that affects the team as they go into the retrospective? For example, are there rumors of layoffs? Has there been a recent merger? A canceled product?

- What are the relationships between team members—how is their work interdependent? What are their personal connections and working relationships?

- What are team members feeling? What are their concerns or anxieties? What are they excited about?

- What kind of outcome will achieve value for the time invested—both for the retrospective sponsor and the team?

- How has the team worked with facilitators before?

The information you glean by exploring these topics will help you formulate a possible goal for the retrospective. It will also help you understand the dynamics of the team, and help you establish relationships if you don't already know people.

2.2 Shaping the Goal for the Retrospective

A useful goal helps answer the question, what will achieve value for the time invested?

A useful goal provides a sense of why people are investing their time, without predetermining what actions or direction the team will take after the retrospective. A restrictive goal acts as a blinder. Choose a broad goal that leaves open possibilities for your team to think creatively about their experiences and discover the insights that are important to them. Unlike more general goals, here you want to avoid goals that define a specific measurable outcome. A goal such as "Determine how to persuade HR to eliminate performance appraisals" blocks consideration of other channels for action or other big issues facing your team.

Here's a goal that's broader but still inappropriate: "Determine what went wrong with testing." A goal like this may send your team in the wrong direction or may open the door for blame.

Useful goals for retrospectives include the following:

- Find ways to improve our practices.

- Discover what we were doing well.

- Understand reasons behind missed targets.

- Find ways to improve our responsiveness to customers.

- Rebuild damaged relationships.

These are just examples. Consider your context, and work with your team to discover a goal that will help your team.

"Continuous process improvement" may work for a couple of iterations. After that, it's stale. Switch to a different goal. After you've considered the context, propose a goal to the team. If the team doesn't buy into the goal, ask the team to describe a goal.

2.3   Determining Duration

How long should your retrospective be?

It depends.

Fifteen minutes can be enough—or not. There's no set formula. Base the length of the retrospective on four factors:

- Length of the iteration

- Complexity (of the technology, relationships with external departments, organization of the team)

- Size of the team

- Level of conflict or controversy

An hour-long retrospective can be enough for a one-week iteration; a half day may be enough for thirty days worth of work. Shortcutting time means cheating results. (Release and end-of-project retrospectives last longer: at least one day and up to four days in some cases.)

Complexity can be about the technical environment, or it can be about relationships. Add more time when there's bound to be lots of discussion.

Add more time for more people. When more than 15 people are in the room everything takes longer.

Projects that fail and projects beset by politics generate controversy on the team and outside the team. Plan on more time for venting by team members.

You can always end the retrospective early if people identify meaningful improvements and finish their plans before the planned end time. There's no point prolonging the retrospective once the team has achieved the goal. But too much time usually isn't the problem. If your team produces only superficial insights and shallow plans, it may be that they need more time.

How Long Does it Take to Prepare for a Retrospective?

The first time you attempt a retrospective that goes beyond asking "What went well?" and "What should we do differently?" it will take time to prepare.

How much time? The first time, it may take as much time as the planned duration of the retrospective. You'll need time to determine the goal, decide on logistics, select activities, and prepare to lead the retrospective. For an hour-long retrospective, you may spend one hour preparing.

Each time after that, you'll need less time to prepare. You'll never get to zero preparation time—that would mean you're not thinking about it at all. But with practice and a collection of activities you feel comfortable with, you'll be able to prepare quickly.

Likewise, preparing for the first full-day retrospective after a release or at the end of the project will need a substantial time investment. This makes sense. If you're going to ask five to twenty people to spend a day learning together, you want to make sure you have a session that will make good use of their time and achieve the desired result.

2.4 Structuring a Retrospective

In Chapter 1, *Helping Your Team Inspect and Adapt*, on page 1, we laid out a structure: Set the Stage, Gather Data, Generate Insights, Decide What to Do and Close the Retrospective. This structure brings in perspectives from all team members, follows a natural order for processing information, and moves the group toward committed action.

You've decided how much time you need to achieve the retrospective goal; now what do you do with that time?

Here's how it might work for a two-hour retrospective:

Set the stage	5%	6 minutes
Gather data	30–50%	40 minutes
Generate insights	20–30%	25 minutes
Decide what to do	15–20%	20 minutes
Close the retrospective	10%	12 minutes
Shuffle time	10–15%	17 minutes
Total	100%	120 minutes

You'll need time to cover all the phases. Plus, people need time to move from one activity to another, so build in "shuffle time."

Tip 2: Time for a Break

Take breaks when there is a logical stopping point, when energy drops, or when people express a need. For retrospectives longer than two hours, build time for breaks into the schedule. Count on a ten-minute (minimum) break every ninety minutes or so.

If you're doing an iteration retrospective, you may be using your team room. The advantages of using your team room are that the artifacts are all there and it feels like business as usual. This is good, except when it isn't.

Change rooms when you need a fresh perspective—for an abnormal iteration termination, for missing an iteration goal, or for an unproductive conflict within the team. Events like these aren't business as usual (at least we hope not), and moving to a different setting makes that clear symbolically. Changing rooms can even help when your retrospectives have gone stale. Most of us have had the experience of driving or walking a familiar route and arriving at our destination without noticing anything along the way. The same process can happen when teams always meet in the same room. Moving to a different room can help people notice different things.

Find a room large enough to accommodate your team without crowding. One way to judge the room size is to look at the occupancy rating. Most conference rooms in corporate buildings (and hotel meeting facilities) have one. Ask the facilities person, and choose a room rated for three to four times the number of people you expect to attend if you are in the United States. (Room ratings are different in other parts of the world.) You want enough space so people can move comfortably—they won't be seated in rows the whole time (we hope they won't be in rows at all).

A circle or semicircle of chairs encourages participation because people can see each other. Classroom or theater-style arrangements stifle participation. Staring at the back of someone else's head isn't conducive to conversation. Tables can be a physical barrier that becomes a psychological barrier. Avoid rooms with an immovable conference table in the middle. That big ol' table will inhibit creative collaboration. This isn't a board meeting, after all.

Tables arranged in a U-shape with a big gulf in the middle create distance and make it hard to move around. If you have to have tables, make sure you can move them.

The key is to move people closer together rather than farther apart and to make it easy for people to see data charts, flip charts, and other information posted during the retrospective.

In addition, facilities folks twitch when you start taping over expensive artwork. Whatever furniture arrangement you choose, find a room that has one long blank wall to post timelines, charts, and flip chart pages. If you can't find a room with a blank wall, look for alternate ways to hang flip charts: two options are to turn tables (*Improvising Space for a Timeline* [Dav05]) on their sides or hang a clothesline (*Re: Improvising Space for a Timeline* [Hin05]). You can also use the open floor spaces to spread out flip pages so people can walk by and view them. When there's nowhere else to hang paper, tape it to the windows (but don't use invisible plastic tape; it's really hard to remove).

Portable white boards are great for capturing small amounts of information. The downside is that once the white board is full, it's erased. That's fine for transient information, but if the team needs the information for the remainder of the retrospective, use a flip chart.

Here's how one retrospective leader thought about a retrospective for his team. The scenario: The team is using some XP practices, though they haven't been pair programming or holding regular retrospectives. The team is in their sixth two-week iteration. This iteration, they met the iteration goal but only by working overtime—violating their agreement to work at a sustainable pace. On top of that, their build system broke during the second week of the iteration.

Given how the iteration went, one of the team members suggested that they'd benefit from examining what happened and making changes in the next iteration. The rest of the team agreed. They want to use their first retrospective to learn from the mishaps and mistakes of the iteration.

Decision: What is the goal?

Learn from mishaps on the previous iteration, uncover root causes of those problems.

Decision: Who will attend?

The team.

Decision: How long?

Two-and-a-half hours. The first retrospective may take longer because we're unfamiliar with this style of discussion. Also, we've been working for twelve weeks and for these issues, we'll need to look back further than the our previous two-week iteration.

Decision: Where do we hold the retrospective?

A conference room that can comfortably hold twenty people. People need to be able to move around for small group work.

Decision: How will we set up the room?

Move the tables to the side of the room. Start seated in a semicircle facing the long wall and then move to the corners of the room for small group work. We don't want people seated around a conference table. The semicircle will allow everyone to see each other for the initial discussion. We'll need variety and space for people to move around.

By now, you should have answers to these questions:

- What is the context surrounding the retrospective?
- What is the goal for this retrospective?
- How long will the retrospective be?
- Where will we hold the retrospective?
- What's the basic structure?

2.5 Selecting Activities

After you have the bare bones of the retrospective—the goal, duration, attendees, room, and setup—it's time to think about activities. Activities are timeboxed processes that help the team move through the phases of the retrospective. Activities provide structure to help your team think together and have several advantages over freewheeling discussion.

Activities do the following:

Encourage Equal Participation   With more than five people it's hard for everyone to participate in a conversation. Working in smaller groups makes it more likely that people will hear and be heard.

Focus the Conversation   Activities have a particular goal that frames the conversation. That reduces (but does not eliminate) the chance of tangential drift.

Encourage New Perspectives   Activities bring people outside their day-to-day modes of thinking and can encourage new ideas. Activities don't have to be elaborate or involved to be effective. Examples of activities that are useful in retrospectives include Brainstorming, Voting with Dots, doing Check-Ins, and performing Pair Interviews.

Choose activities that support the goal of the retrospective. If there's no way to discuss the activity that makes a connection between the activity and the work, omit it. We're not against games and simulations—in fact we use them often—when they serve a purpose and move the retrospective forward. Ice-breakers, energizers, and games that don't relate to the work don't fit in retrospectives. There's only so much time, so don't waste it with activities that are "just for fun." Have fun, but have a purpose.

J. M. Keller, an expert in motivation and learning, developed criteria for evaluating instructional designs. The criteria are Attention, Relevance, Confidence/Competence, Satisfaction—ARCS for short (*Strategies for Stimulating the Motivation to Learn* [Kel87]). While you aren't developing instructional material, you are creating an environment for learning. The same criteria apply. If you did interviews as up-front work, you may have some clues about which will be relevant to your team.

Choose activities that help people stay engaged so they don't drift off (Attention) and that are relevant to the goal (Relevance). You want activities that people can accomplish successfully (Confident/Competence). Avoid activities that are designed to make people feel stupid, inept, or set up. People usually become angry when they feel set up and become defensive if they feel they're looking or acting like dummies. That's not what you want in a retrospective. Finally, make sure activities fit into the overall design so people think the retrospective is a good use of their time (Satisfaction).

Vary activities to keep your team engaged. Follow a pair activity with one that involves a small group or the whole group. Alternate sedentary activities with ones where people move.

After a while, the same old activities lose their zest. If you're bored with an activity, chances are your team is, too. Find new activities to keep your team (and yourself) interested. When people are interested, they're less likely to fall into habitual thinking—and you don't want habitual thinking. You want creative thinking. After you've been leading retrospectives for a while, you'll start making up your own activities. Many activities for generating ideas, analyzing problems, or identifying novel solutions can be adapted for retrospectives. In the meanwhile, we've included activities for each phase of the retrospective with step-by-step guidelines (see the "Activities" chapters).

Tip 3:   Have a Backup

Choose two activities for each stage—one short and one long. Substitute the shorter activity if time is tight.

Now, we'll look at selecting activities for each phase. We'll pick up the scenario of the XP team who has been working over time to meet goals and whose build system broke down. (Each of these activities is described in detail in the "Activities" chapters that follow.)

Phase: Set the Stage

Activity: Focus On/Focus Off

Why? After the opening (review goal, schedule, and working agreements), this activity will help establish a mind-set of looking at the issues without assigning blame. We want to foster open discussion.

Phase: Gather the Data

Activity: Timeline with Color Code Dots

Why? The team is looking at a fairly long period of time and this will help them remember what happened in earlier iterations. It will help people see connections between events. Color coding will help us see facts and feeling and will be an efficient use of time.

Phase: Generate Insights

Activity: Patterns and Shifts

Why? I'll guide the group to recognize and name patterns and significant events contributing to our current problems.

Activity: Fishbone

Why? After looking at the patterns, we need to determine root causes. We'll analyze significant events and factors behind the problems.

Activity: Report Out and Synthesis

Why? We need to share the work from small groups and look for common threads and common causes.

Why? If the underlying issues can't be solved in the team, we need to create an influence strategy to show our manager why it's important to fix the problem.

Phase: Decide What to Do

Activity: Prioritize with Dots

Why? We need to identify the top two to three root causes to work on starting in the next iteration. We can't absorb a long list of changes; we need to work on the things that will make the biggest difference.

The next step depends on what the team identifies as the most important thing to work on.

Option 1: Write story cards (Retrospective Planning Game).

Why? We can take the story card items into our next iteration planning meeting and incorporate them into the rest of our work.

Option 2: Add working agreements.

Why? The team may need some more relevant working agreements (since they've been violating the ones they have now), and we can do that right in the session.

Option 3: Write a proposal.

Phase: Close the Retrospective

Activity: +/Delta

Why? Improve the retrospective.

Activity: Appreciations

Why? Provide an opportunity for people to acknowledge contributions. We need a lift after a tough iteration and hard work in the retrospective. Note to self: remember to thank the team for their hard work.

Figure 3, *The retrospective leader's notes*, on page 25 shows the retrospective leader's notes for the session. Figure 4, *Retrospective agenda*, on page 26 shows the agenda poster for the retrospective.

Suppose this design was for your retrospective.

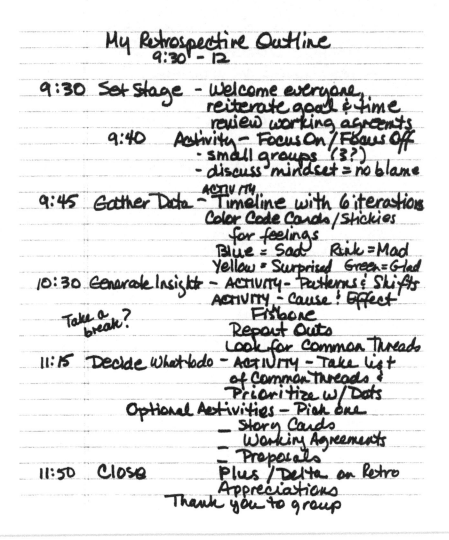

My Retrospective Outline
9:30 - 12

9:30 Set Stage - Welcome everyone,
            reiterate goal & time
            review working agreements
    9:40   Activity - Focus On / Focus Off
            - small groups (3?)
            - discuss mindset = no blame

9:45 Gather Data - ACTIVITY
            Timeline with 6 iterations
            Color Code Cards / Stickies
                for feelings
            Blue = Sad   Pink = Mad
            Yellow = Surprised Green = Glad
10:30 Generate Insights - ACTIVITY - Patterns & Shifts
            ACTIVITY - Cause & Effect
Take a ?   Fishbone
break?   Report Outs
            Look for Common Threads
11:15 Decide What to do - ACTIVITY - Take list
            of Common Threads &
            Prioritize w/ Dots
    Optional Activities - Pick one
            - Story Cards
            - Working Agreements
            - Proposals
11:50 Close   Plus / Delta on Retro
            Appreciations
            Thank you to group

Figure 3—The retrospective leader's notes

You know the goal for the retrospective, how long it will be, where the session will be, who will attend, and the activities you'll use to help the group think and solve problems together.

Now all you have to do is stand up and lead the group.

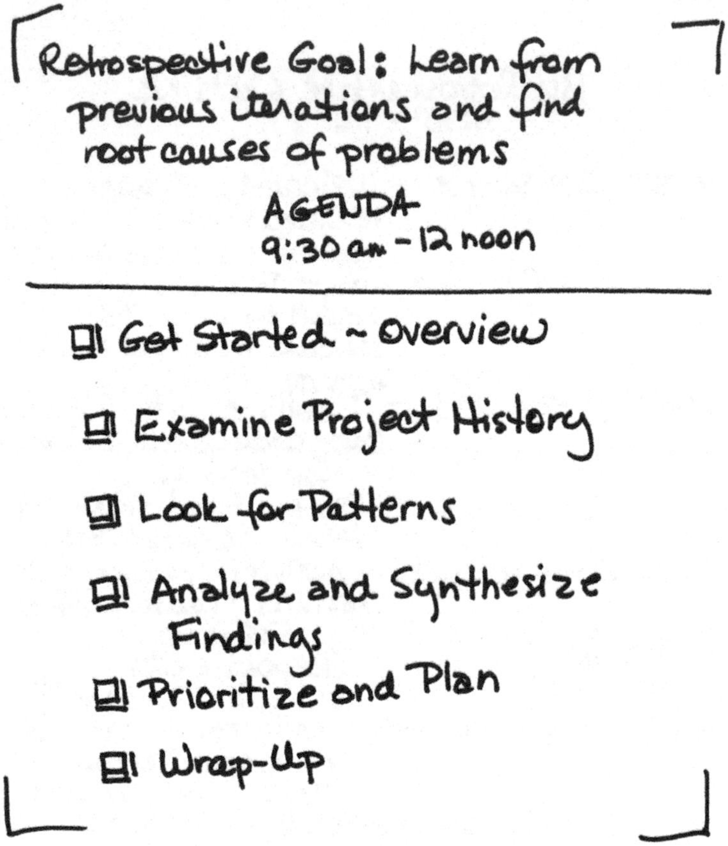

Retrospective Goal: Learn from
previous iterations and find
root causes of problems
    AGENDA
    9:30 am – 12 noon
_____

☑ Get Started ~ Overview

☑ Examine Project History

☑ Look for Patterns

☑ Analyze and Synthesize
    Findings
☑ Prioritize and Plan

☑ Wrap-Up

The items cover all five phases of a retrospective.

Figure 4—Retrospective agenda

CHAPTER 3

Leading Retrospectives

This chapter is about the role and skills of a retrospective leader. You don't need to be a professional facilitator to lead an iteration retrospective, but you do need basic facilitation skills. To learn the skills, you need to understand the role, practice, and seek feedback.

As a retrospective facilitator you may follow the content, but your primary responsibility is the process. When facilitators talk about process, they aren't talking about a heavyweight methodology. *Process* means managing activities, managing group dynamics, and managing time (*The Skilled Facilitator* [Sch94]). Retrospective leaders focus on the process and structure of the retrospective. They attend to the needs and dynamics of the group and help the group reach a goal. Retrospective leaders remain neutral in discussions, even when they have strong opinions.

When the content involves your own team, it's easy to get caught up in the discussion. It's tempting to jump into an engaging conversation, especially when you care about the topic. But, if you're immersed in the content, you can't pay full attention to the process. Wait a beat to determine whether your thoughts are necessary. Most often, your team will do nicely without your input. The risk of giving input is that when the leader jumps in too often, it quashes group discussion.

Participants, on the other hand, focus on the content, discuss, sometimes disagree (though not disagreeably), and make decisions. Participants aim toward a goal and manage their own thoughts, feelings, and responses so they contribute positively to the conversations and outcome.

Tip 4: When to Offer Content Expertise

You may have important content to offer that no one else in the group has. When that happens, tell the team you are leaving the retrospective leader role temporarily to contribute to the discussion. Hand your marker to another team member to symbolize that you are not in the facilitator role while you participate. (Just make sure you get the marker—and your role—back.)

3.1 Managing Activities

Every retrospective design includes activities—such as creating working agreements, building a timeline, brainstorming, and prioritizing—to help the team think together. You'll need to introduce each activity, monitor the room during the activity, and debrief the activity when it's done.

Most people want to know something about the purpose of an activity before they begin. Give a broad sense of the territory the team will explore without revealing the details of what will happen or specifying what the team will learn.

Tip 5: Introducing Activities

The first time you use an activity, write a script so that you remember what to say and don't garble the instructions or leave something out.

Once you have your script, practice saying it aloud. Saying the words is different from reading them or thinking them. As you hear yourself give the instruction, you'll notice where you stumble and where even you can't follow the instructions. Then you can refine your script and practice again.

You may not follow the script in the end, but preparing and practicing will help you describe the activity clearly and concisely.

Here's an introduction for an activity to re-create the timeline of a release: "To understand our iteration we need to tell the whole story from everyone's perspective. We'll create a timeline that shows events that happened during the project. After we have a timeline as complete as it can be for now, we'll look for interesting patterns and explore puzzles."

This tells you about the territory of "understand our iteration," and lists the steps at a high level: "create the timeline," "look for interesting patterns," and "explore puzzles." It doesn't tell your team exactly what the outcome will be. That's for the team to create.

Most people (even really smart people) can't absorb detailed instructions for a multipart activity. Give the details for each part, just in time. For the timeline the details of the first steps are as follows: "Let's get into groups of two or three. In your group, brainstorm all the events that took place during the release. An event doesn't have to be a milestone—it can be anything that happened on the project." After giving the instructions, ask for questions about the task. Pause. Count to ten. Someone will have a question—wait for it.

As the retrospective leader, you have two tasks during an activity: be available to answer questions about the activity, and monitor the room.

While the group is working on an activity, listen to the noise level. Lots of conversation is an indication of good energy. It's also a clue that people are done with a quiet activity or need more time for a discussion activity. For an activity that involves writing or individual work, conversational buzz indicates that people are done and have started talking to their neighbor. If it sounds like there's still lively conversation at the end of a discussion activity, check to see whether people need more time. Of course, the sound of lively conversation may mean that people have finished the task and are talking about the latest movie.

Debrief every activity. A debrief helps your team examine their experience and extract insights. They'll make conscious connections and form new ideas. Debriefing each activity builds toward the insights and decisions of the retrospective.

So, it's important to debrief. Now how do you do it?

Here's a simple, four-step method to debrief almost any activity (*The Art of Focused Conversation: 100 Ways to Access Group Wisdom in the Workplace* [Sta97]):

1. Start by asking for observable events and sensory input. "What did you see and hear?"

2. Ask how people responded to those events and inputs. "What surprised you? Where were you challenged?"

3. Ask for insights and analysis with questions, like "What insight do you have about this?" followed by "What does this tell you about our project?" These questions help people formulate their ideas and connect the activity to the project.

4. After you've established the link between the activity and the project, complete the learning cycle by asking group members how they will apply their insights: "What's one thing you might do differently?"

Notice anything familiar about this? If follows the same flow as the retrospective structure (gather data, both facts and feelings; generate insights; and decide what to do).

There are lots of other ways to debrief (see Appendix 2, *Debriefing Activities*, on page 145 for additional ideas). This is a good place to start.

For a five- to twenty-minute activity, spend 50–100% as much time on debriefing as on the activity. So for a ten-minute activity, allow five to ten minutes for debriefing.

3.2 Managing Group Dynamics

Most of the time managing group dynamics in a retrospective means managing participation: making sure people who have something to say have the chance and making sure people who have a lot to say don't dominate. Watch out for people who are talking more (or much less) than others. Make an opening for the quieter team members by asking to hear other opinions. Notice when someone looks as though he or she was about to speak but was cut off. Ask whether he or she has something to say. Create an opportunity without putting people on the spot or demanding an answer (*How to Improve Meetings When You're Not in Charge* [Der03]).

To draw out quieter people, try saying something like "We haven't heard Leigh and Venkat yet. What would you add?" Be willing to accept a pass.

If someone just won't shut up, be direct (in private). If you've observed the pattern, talk to the person before the retrospective. Describe your observations, and describe the impact on the team—other people have stopped participating. Ask him or her to hold back. If the private conversation doesn't work, be direct in the retrospective. When one team member is first to speak on every question, hold up a hand and say, "We've heard from you on every question; let's hear from some other people." Keep your tone neutral. An emphatic delivery—"We've HEARD from YOU on EVERY question"—conveys blame and won't help the retrospective.

Managers won't be in every retrospective, but when they are, they are particularly prone to dominating the conversation. It's not always their fault—if team members hold back when a manager is in the room (for whatever reason), the manager tends to fill the dead air. Meet with managers before the retrospective. Coach them on appropriate participation. Ask them to let others talk first, acknowledge the contributions others make, and be careful how they disagree. "I see it differently" preserves participation. Statements like "You're wrong," "You just don't understand," "You're not listening to me," and "I disagree" quash participation or lead to confrontation. Neither one is good.

Here's how one retrospective leader handled a talkative manager: Rajiv, a project manager was a high-energy, verbal guy. And he was excited about the project. Jess met with him before the retrospective to discuss participation. Rajiv worried he'd forget to wait for others to speak first. Jess and Rajiv agreed on a signal: if he spoke out of turn, Jess would walk over and stand next to him. They never used the signal. Just knowing it was there was enough to help Rajiv wait.

Tip 6: Strategies for Helping Your Team Move Forward

Sometimes teams become stuck. When that happens, you have options as a retrospective leader.

You can help restore their creative juices by asking questions such as these:

- What have we tried before? What happened? What would you like to happen differently?

- If we had that, what would we gain?

- Have you ever tried this a different way? What happened?

You can ask for more opinions, especially from people who have been thinking more than talking.

You can suggest additional research before committing to a solution.

You can take off the retrospective leader hat and offer content knowledge from personal experience.

You could tell the team what to do, but only if you want to cheat their learning.

After managing participation, the next most common issues are violating working agreements and blaming. Both have negative effects, so you don't want to let them pass unnoticed.

Sooner or later, a team member will violate a working agreement. Humans have good intentions but fall back into old patterns. When they do, remind your team of their working agreements. If you allow violations to continue without comment, team members get the message that working agreements are optional. Optional working agreements have no value. It's everyone's job to monitor working agreements.

Blame starts a downward spiral of defensiveness and counterblame that will torpedo a retrospective. Listen for "you" language ("You broke the build!") and labeling statements ("You're immature!"). Both signal blame. Blame hurts the retrospective by distracting attention from real problems.

Encourage "I" language. "I" language centers on the speaker's observation and experience, rather than labeling the other person. When you hear blame or personal criticism, intervene and redirect the discussion to the content.

Here's how one retrospective leader handled a blame: during the platform expansion retrospective, one team member blamed another for breaking the build. "We'd have met our target if it weren't for you!"

"Hold on!" the retrospective leader said, "can you say that using `I'? language?" The team member thought for a while and then said, "I am angry that we missed our target because we had so much trouble fixing the build." Then the team was able to look at bigger issues with the build without blaming one individual.

Describe what you've seen and heard: "I'm hearing labels and `you' language." Describing the behavior causes people to pause and consider what they're doing.

Group dynamics include team member interactions and emotions. You aren't responsible for other people's emotions, but as retrospective leader, you are responsible for keeping the session productive. And that means you need to be prepared to handle emotional interactions and situations.

Most interactions and emotions help the group move forward. Some don't. Here are some challenging group dynamics and interactions to watch out for—and what to do about them. With any luck you won't encounter all of these in one retrospective ;-). If outbursts are the rule on your team, something else is happening. Retrospectives can't solve every problem; if the issue is deeper than normal team friction, contact your HR representative for resources and guidance.

When people have been bottling up their emotions, they come out in funny ways: people cry, shout, stomp out of the room, laugh hysterically, or clown when the topic is serious.

Before you jump in to fix things, notice your own response. It's easy to focus on comforting one person and lose track of the goal and the needs of the team. In a retrospective, your primary responsibility is to the interactions of the team as a whole, not to individuals. That doesn't mean ignoring what's going on with individual emotions; it means dealing with emotions in a way that is helpful and respectful to the team and the individual.

Here are some strategies that have worked for us and can work for you. Having a mental picture of how you'll respond gives you more options in the moment. So, think of the outburst that scares you the most, and mentally rehearse using one of these strategies. Outbursts are unsettling, but they don't have to derail the process. If you think you could never do something like this, remember that one of the Retrospective Goddesses started out as a programmer.

Tears   Offer a box of tissues. When the person is able to speak, ask, "What is happening for you? Can you share it with the group?" Pause. Given time, the person often shares something heartfelt (and usually relevant) about the topic under discussion.

Shouting   In most places, when someone starts shouting, the rest of the people in the room stop participating. And that makes it unproductive for everyone. Intervene immediately. Hold up one hand as a stop sign, and say calmly but forcefully, "Hold it." Then say, "I want to hear what you have to say, and I can't when you're shouting. Can you tell us why without shouting?" Don't be surprised if the person responds, "I'm not shouting!" When someone is upset or excited, he or she may not be aware of the rising vocal volume. There's no need to say "Yes, you are." Calling attention to the yelling is usually enough to stop it.

If your team member continues to blame or yell, call a break, and talk to the person privately. Let him or her know how the behavior is affecting the group. Ask for agreement to express emotion in a nonthreatening way. If the person is unwilling, ask (don't tell) him or her to leave and return when he or she has more self-control.

Stomping Out   When a team member stomps out, let him or her go. Ask the team, "What just happened?" They will have an idea. Ask whether it is possible to continue without the person who left. Most of the time, they'll say they can continue, though they may need to talk about the departure.

If this happens more than once, another issue is at play. Talk to the individual outside the retrospective.

Inappropriate Laughter and Clowning   It is great to have fun in a retrospective. And people may use laughter and humor to deflect from a sensitive topic. When the laughter has an edge or your team repeatedly avoids a topic, it's time to step in. Make an observation, and ask a question: "I've noticed that every time we get near this topic, someone tells a joke. What's happening?" They'll tell you and engage the topic.

Also watch for two other types of situations. They aren't outbursts, but they are worth noticing.

Uncharacteristic Silence   When a team that has been voluble goes quiet, something is going on. Again, step in with an observation and a question: "It seems to me that the group is being awfully quiet. There was a lot of energy and conversation earlier. What's going on now?" Your team may just be tired and need a break. Or they may be unsure how to approach a topic. Once you ask the question, someone will figure out how to broach the topic, and the proverbial dam will burst.

Of course, the fact that a team goes quiet may not mean anything. They may be thinking, tired, or simply a quiet group. When the silence is sudden or out of character, it's a clue worth following.

Currents Beneath the Surface   Fidgeting and intense side conversations may indicate something going on just beneath the surface. Again, ask the group what is going on. They will tell you.

Here's how one retrospective leader handled a sudden disturbance in a retrospective: During an off-site release retrospective for a team building network infrastructure, Lindsey noticed the manager take a call on his cell phone, even though the working agreements prohibited calls. He left. When he came back in the room, he had a quiet side conversation with one person, then another. Laptops opened. Everyone was still trying to track the discussion in the room, but something was distracting them. Lindsey stopped the discussion and asked, "What's happening?" A team member explained that there was a crisis back at the office and the sales manager wanted them to come back and fix it. They wanted to stay in the session but were distracted by his request and perceived urgency for the customer. Lindsey and the team discussed their options: stop the retrospective and reschedule it, ignore the request, or try to do something from where they were. The team set a timebox for immediate problem solving in the room and then resumed the retrospective.

Lindsey didn't blame anyone for not following the agreements. In most cases, naming the behavior, commenting on it, and asking the group what's happening will diffuse the situation and shift the dynamic.

Whew! After all that, managing time will be easy!

3.3 Managing Time

Here's the rub: when you're leading a retrospective, you should respond to the needs of the group, *and* you need to pay attention to time and stay within the timebox all at once. It's a dilemma.

Bring a timepiece that will allow you to time activities. We sometimes lose track of time, so we'll often jot down the start time so we know when to end an activity. Or you can use a stopwatch to time activities.

If you're working with a group much larger than eight people, you'll need a way to cue people that it's time to move to another step. Use a bell, chime, or some other not-too-obnoxious sound when it's time to come together as a group, debrief, or provide additional instructions for an activity. Yelling over the group isn't effective and sends the wrong message. Whistling works to gain attention, but not always with the desired effect. Duck calls, cow sounds, and other animal sounds work in groups of less than ten (the sound doesn't carry in larger groups), but well... they don't add to your dignity (if you care about such things).

When the discussion still has energy yet the time you've planned has run out, ask the group what they want to do: "I'm concerned that if we continue this discussion we won't meet our end goal. What do you want to do?" The group will refocus and move ahead, or they will tell you this conversation is more important than the original goal. Put the decision in the hands of the group.

Usually it's pretty clear. When it's not, look for a compromise such as timeboxing the discussion or agreeing to revisit the topic later (in the retrospective or afterward).

Be prepared to swap to a shorter activity if time is running short. You still have the responsibility to meet the goal of the retrospective—identify and plan for experiments and improvements.

3.4 Managing You

In addition to managing activities, group dynamics, and time, you need to manage you.

Staying aware of all these team and interpersonal dynamics may seem overwhelming. The key to managing group dynamics is not technique (although it helps to have strategies) but in understanding and managing your own emotional state and responses. If you aren't managing your own state, no technique or strategy will help. When emotions are high, your team needs someone to stay outside the turmoil. That someone is you, the retrospective leader.

If you feel your anxiety or tension rising, take a deep breath. Call a break if you need to do so. Your anxiety is a clue that you need to sort out what to do next to serve the group. Remember, you didn't cause the emotions in the room, and you don't have responsibility to make everything and everyone happy and nice.

During the break, take a moment to shake out your hands and feet to release tension and get your blood flowing again. Take three deep breaths. This may seem like superfluous advice; but when people are tense and anxious, it reduces blood flow to the brain... which reduces the ability to think clearly, which contributes to anxiety and tension. You see the picture. Oxygen to the brain is a good thing. It helps you think. Once your brain is oxygenated, ask yourself these questions:

- "What just happened?"

- "How much was inside me, and how much was outside me?"

- "How did the group get here?"

- "Where does the group need to go next?"

- "What are three options I have for next steps?"

- "What will I offer the group?"

These questions will help you re-center. And then you can use one of the strategies for managing group dynamics. As long as you have a strategy, you won't have to stand there frozen, not knowing what to do. Over time, your comfort in dealing with charged emotional situations will grow. Find a mentor whom you have seen manage emotions in groups. Work with your mentor to gain confidence and learn more options for handling emotional situations. And remember to breathe.

3.5   Taking Your Skills to the Next Level

If you enjoy helping groups think together, increase your skills as a facilitator and augment your toolbox. Consider deepening your skills in these areas:

- Working with activities. There's an art to developing, introducing, and debriefing activities and simulations to help people think and learn together. In addition to using activities in retrospectives, using activities and simulations is helpful if coaching, teaching, or training is part of your job.

- Helping groups reach decisions. There's a huge body of knowledge related to how people really make decisions (it's not entirely by logic, by the way). You can improve the quality of decision making in your group by knowing what decision process fits the situation and how to help the group converge on a decision.

- Understanding and managing group dynamics. Learning about people and people in groups is a lifelong study. Your skills in this area will help you build and nurture high-performing groups as well as run a darn good retrospective.

- Increasing self-awareness. Self-awareness is the foundation of personal effectiveness. You can't go wrong learning more about yourself and learning how you respond under stress. Gaining awareness of habitual patterns is the first step to being able to choose an appropriate response rather than simply reacting.

- Creating and using flip charts. Don't use any more of those scribbled flip charts that no one can read from more than a foot away! If you work with groups, learning how to present information visually helps the group process information quickly and efficiently.

These skills apply in many situations, not just retrospectives. Your understanding of group process and your ability to help groups succeed will help you succeed, too.

Practice facilitating other kinds of meetings. If you belong to a volunteer group or some other organization outside of work, offer to facilitate a meeting or subcommittee. It's low risk and will give you experience. Practice in managing the dynamics of any meeting will pay off in managing the dynamics in a retrospective.

Observe other people who are effective at leading meetings and working with groups. Watch how they interact with people and how they respond when a session isn't going smoothly. You may not want to use someone else's exact words, but you can analyze what you see and adapt it to fit your own style.

Practice with feedback is the best way to learn facilitation skills (*Climbing the learning curve: Practice with feedback* [Der02]). Ask someone you trust (and who has some facilitation awareness) to observe as you facilitate. If you have a specific area you want to learn about, ask your observer to pay special attention to that aspect of your facilitation. Or you may ask your trusted observer to look for areas where he or she senses you have habits you aren't aware of.

For resources on increasing your facilitation skills, see Appendix 4, *Resources for Learning Facilitation Skills*, on page 149.

You are probably an expert at what you do now. Facilitation draws on different skills than most of us develop working in software. Facilitation also requires a different perspective. It takes time and practice to feel comfortable with new skills. Give yourself time, manage your expectations, and find mentors. You'll inspect and adapt your facilitation, too.

CHAPTER 4

Activities to Set the Stage

Setting the stage prepares the team for the work they'll do in the retrospective. Setting the stage can be as simple as reviewing the goal, reviewing the agenda, checking in, and reviewing working agreements. When the group needs to do more work to be ready to work, use these activities.

Also see the activity Temperature Reading on page 114 and Figure 21, *The Elements of Temperature Reading*, on page 115.

4.1 Activity: Check-In

Use this to set the stage in an iteration retrospective.

Purpose

Help people put aside other concerns and focus on the retrospective. Help people articulate what they want from the retrospective.

Time needed

Five to ten minutes, depending on the size of the group.

Description

After welcoming the participants and reviewing the goal and agenda, the retrospective leader asks one brief question. Each person answers in round-robin fashion.

Steps

1. Ask one question that each person can answer with a word or short phrase.

   Here are possible questions:

   What is one word that describes what you need for yourself from this session?

   In one or two words, what is happening for you right now?

   In a word or two, what are your hopes for the retrospective?

   What is one thing that's on your mind?

   Note: If you use this question, also ask what each person needs to do to set the concern aside. Sometimes writing the concern down and putting it in a book or pocket—literally setting it aside—helps people set the concern aside mentally.

   Coming into this retrospective, if you were a car, what kind of car would you be?

   Note: you can use many different metaphors with this question—type of animal, hardware, flavor. But be careful not to use a metaphor that will seem frivolous or silly to your team.

   It's OK for people to say "I pass" on any question. Even saying "I pass" will make sure their voice is heard in the room.

2. Go around the room listening to each person's answer. You may thank each person (be sure to thank every person if you do). Refrain from offering evaluative comments such as "good" or "wonderful."

Materials and preparation

Prepare and choose a question ahead of time.

Examples

Some teams identify four to five emotions words, for example *happy, angry, apprehensive, sad,* and *hopeful.* Each team member checks in by reporting his or her emotional state using one of these words. Using this type of check-in is helpful when there has been conflict or failure—because it makes it OK to have strong feelings related to the events of the iteration.

4.2 Activity: Focus On/Focus Off

Use this to set the stage in an iteration retrospective.

Purpose

Help establish a mind-set for productive communication. Help participants set aside blaming and judgment—and fear of blaming and judgment.

Time needed

Eight to twelve minutes, depending on the size of the group.

Description

After welcoming the participants and reviewing the goal and agenda, the retrospective leader describes productive and unproductive communication patterns. After describing those patterns, the participants discuss what they mean for the retrospective.

Steps

1. Draw attention to the Focus On/Focus Off poster (see Figure 5, *Focus on/Focus off activity*, on page 43) and briefly read through it.
2. Form small groups, with no more than four people per group. Ask each group to take one pair of words to define and describe. If there are more than four pairs/groups, it's OK if more than one group has the same pair of words.
3. Ask each group to discuss what their two words mean and what behaviors they represent. Have them describe the impact each would have on the team and the retrospective.
4. Each group reports on their discussion to the whole team.
5. Ask people whether they are willing to stay in the left column (Focus On descriptions).

Materials and Preparation

Prepare a flip chart with the Focus On/Focus Off terms ahead of time.

Examples

For a release or project retrospective, use this activity as a lead-in to establish working agreements for the retrospective. Many teams carry forward the Focus On behaviors as working agreements to improve their day-to-day communication.

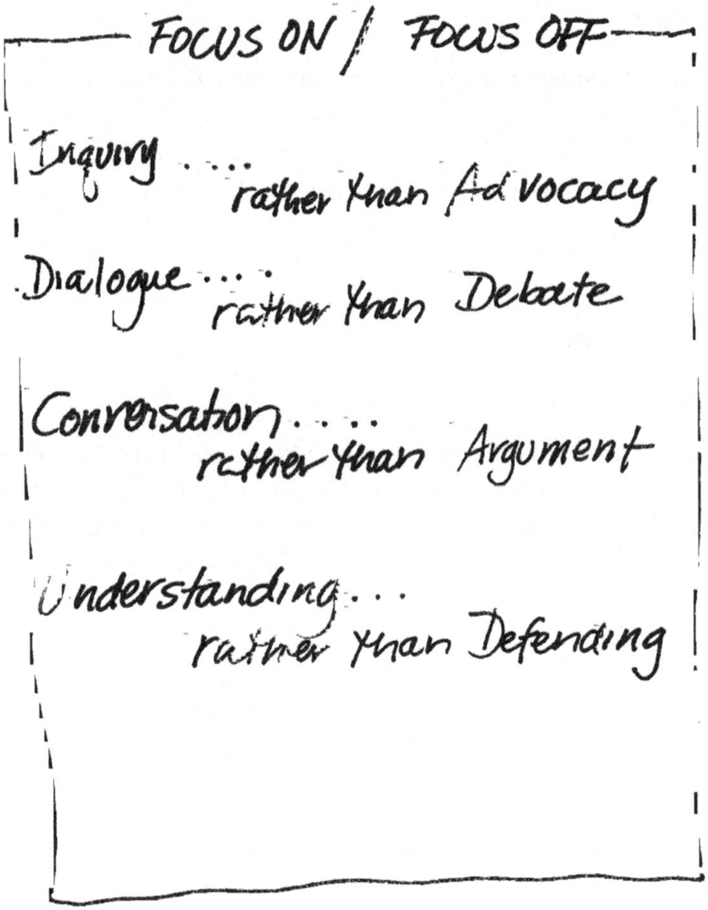

FOCUS ON / FOCUS OFF

Inquiry . . . . rather than Advocacy

Dialogue . . . . rather than Debate

Conversation . . . . rather than Argument

Understanding . . . rather than Defending

This is a great activity to focus attention on behaviors and how they affect the people on the team.

Figure 5—Focus on/Focus off activity

4.3 Activity: ESVP

Use this to set the stage in a longer iteration, release, or project retrospective.

Purpose

Focus people on the work of the retrospective. Understand people's attitudes to the retrospective.

Time needed

Ten to fifteen minutes.

Description

Each participant reports (anonymously) his or her attitude toward the retrospective as an Explorer, Shopper, Vacationer, or Prisoner (ESVP). The retrospective leader collects the results and creates a histogram to show the data, and then guides a discussion about what the results mean for the group.

Steps

1. Explain that you are taking a poll to learn about how people view their participation in the retrospective.

2. Show the flip chart and define the terms:

   - Explorers are eager to discover new ideas and insights. They want to learn everything they can about the iteration/release/project.

   - Shoppers will look over all the available information, and will be happy to go home with one useful new idea.

   - Vacationers aren't interested in the work of the retrospective, but are happy to be away from the daily grind. They may pay attention some of the time, but they are mostly glad to be out of the office.

   - Prisoners feel that they've been forced to attend and would rather be doing something else.

3. Distribute slips of paper or small index cards for people to record their attitude toward learning in the retrospective today. Instruct people to fold their paper in half for privacy.

4. As people finish writing and folding, collect the slips and shuffle them.

5. Ask one of the participants to make tick marks on the histogram as you read the slips. After you read each slip, put them in your pocket. When

you've read all the slips, tear them up and throw them away. Be conspicuous about this so people know that no one will try to identify who responded with what from the handwriting.

6. Ask the group, "What do you make of this data?" Then lead a brief discussion about how the attitudes in the room will affect the retrospective.

7. Debrief by asking "How are these categories like our attitudes toward daily work?"

Materials and Preparation

Voting slips or index cards and pencils or pens.

A flip chart prepared for the histogram.

Examples

If the majority of the people in the room are Vacationers, that's interesting information about how people feel about their work environment. You may want turn on a dime and make that the major topic of discussion for the retrospective!

In the example in Figure 6, *ESVP activity*, on page 46, no one feels like a Prisoner. If you do have Prisoners in the room, suggest that they can choose how they will spend their time... they can engage or not. If they don't engage, the group will be the poorer for it.

If you plan to take a break in your retrospective, suggest that if people choose to return after the break, they are choosing to attend the retrospective—they aren't Prisoners anymore.

If you've done your homework, chances are you won't be surprised by finding a room full of Prisoners. As in the situation with many Vacationers, if the majority of the group feels they are Prisoners, that's what you need to deal with: you won't get anywhere in the retrospective if you don't.

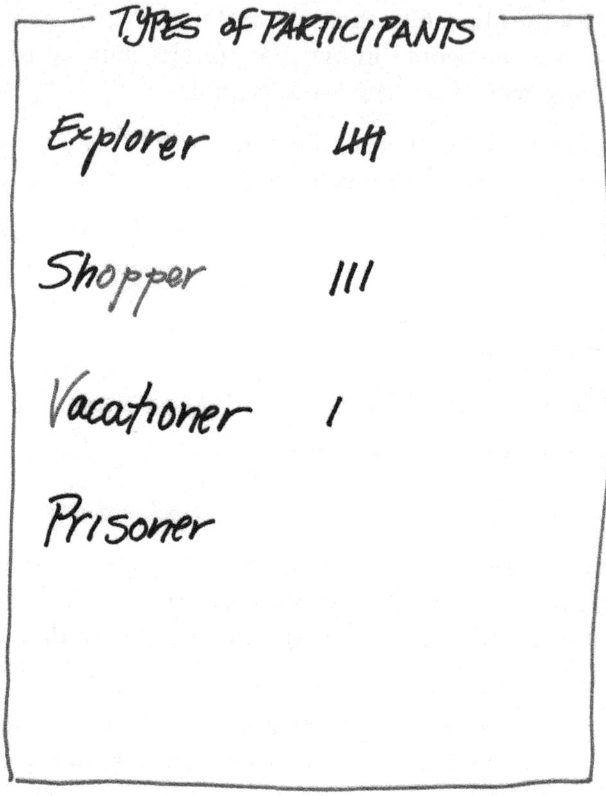

```
┌─────── TYPES of PARTICIPANTS ───────┐
│                                      │
│   Explorer        LHI                │
│                                      │
│                                      │
│   Shopper         |||                │
│                                      │
│                                      │
│   Vacationer       |                 │
│                                      │
│                                      │
│   Prisoner                           │
│                                      │
│                                      │
└──────────────────────────────────────┘
```

Here's a completed histogram from an iteration retrospective. Most of the team is interested in learning from the retrospective (Explorers and Shoppers). There's one Vacationer—and that's OK.

Figure 6—ESVP activity

4.4   Activity: Working Agreements

Use this to set the stage in an iteration, release, or project retrospective.

Purpose

Establish a set of behaviors that will support the team in having productive discussions. Establish that team members are responsible for monitoring their interactions. Provide candidates for day-to-day working agreements if the team doesn't already have them.

Time needed

Ten to thirty minutes, depending on the size of the group.

Description

Team members work together to generate ideas for effective behaviors at work then choose five to seven agreements to guide team interactions or processes.

Steps

After the retrospective leader welcomes the participants and reviews the goal and agenda, the team works in pairs or small groups (no more than four in a group) to develop candidate working agreements. Going around the room, each group reports their most important proposed working agreement. When all the unique proposed working agreements are collected, the retrospective leader helps the group make needed amendments and select three to seven working agreements that will set the standard for behavior during the retrospective.

1. Explain the activity: "We'll develop a set of working agreements for the retrospective so that everyone will know our expectations for working together. It will be each team member's responsibility to follow the agreements and the job of the whole team to notice and bring it to the team's attention when an agreement is violated. The purpose of the agreements is to help us have the discussions we need to have during the retrospective."

2. Form pairs or small groups, no more than four per group.

3. Ask each group to develop three to five working agreements that, if followed, would help the team have productive discussions during the retrospective. Remind the group that these are not for business as

usual—they should be new behaviors or ones that aren't yet normal behavior for the group.

4. In round-robin fashion, ask each group to report their most important agreement and write it on a flip chart page. Write down the exact words used by the team member. Continue until you've captured all the unique proposed agreements.

5. Explain that for the retrospective, the group should choose three to seven agreements. Having more than seven is too hard to remember and follow.

6. If there are fewer than three proposed agreements, ask for clarifying questions for each agreement. When everyone understands, use a consensus "thumb vote" for each agreement. Thumb up = I agree. Thumb sideways = I will support the will of the group. Thumb down = I veto.

7. If there are more than seven proposed agreements, use dot voting to prioritize. Give each team member three color dots to vote with. Each person can put one dot on three separate items, or all dots on one. Use a consensus thumb vote to ratify the top five to seven vote getters.

Materials and Preparation

Flip chart, markers, sticky dots.

Examples

We're often asked for examples of typical working agreements. But we don't see a pattern of agreements. Each team develops working agreements that reflect their unique concerns.

CHAPTER 5

Activities to Gather Data

Gathering data creates a shared picture of what happened during the iteration, release, or project. Without data, the team is speculating on what changes and improvements to make. These activities help the team view and integrate different types of data.

5.1 Activity: Timeline

Use this to gather data in a longer iteration, release, or project retrospective.

Purpose

Stimulate memories of what happened during the increment of work. Create a picture of the work from many perspectives. Examine assumptions about who did what when. See patterns or when energy levels changed. Use this for "just the facts" or facts and feelings.

Time Needed

Thirty to ninety minutes, depending on the size of the group and the length of the increment of work.

Description

Group members write cards to represent memorable, personally meaningful, or otherwise significant events during the iteration, release, or project and then post them in (roughly) chronological order. The retrospective leader supports the team to discuss the events to understand facts and feelings during the iteration, release, or project.

Steps

1. Set up the activity by saying "We'll fill in a timeline to create a fuller picture of this iteration/release/project. We want to see it from many perspectives."

2. Divide the team into small groups, with no more than five in a group. Keep people who worked closely with each other together (affinity groups). It's better to have two small groups representing one affinity than one big group.

   Hand out markers and index cards or sticky notes.

   Make sure each person has a marker. Although it sounds school-marmish, you do need to remind people to write legibly, so people can read the cards.

3. Describe the process.

   Ask people to think back over the iteration/release/project and remember all the memorable, personally meaningful, or significant events and write them down, one per card or sticky note.

Remind the group that the point is to see many perspectives—so they don't arrive at a consensus of what was memorable, meaningful, or significant. If it was any of those to one person, that's enough.

Tell them they have ten minutes for this activity.

If you are color coding (see "Variations") explain what the colors mean and post a legend.

Remind people to write legibly.

4. Monitor the level of activity as people start talking about events and writing cards. If people haven't started writing cards after half the time has elapsed, remind them to start writing. When the groups have a stack of cards, invite people to start posting them (see Figure 7, *A timeline for a retrospective that looked at three iterations*, on page 53).

5. When all the cards are posted, invite the team to walk by the timeline and see what others have posted. It's OK for people to add new cards at this point as they remember more events.

6. Allow a break or take lunch before analyzing the timeline.

Variations

We have collected several variations on the timeline activity. We use index cards, sticky notes, markers and dots in a number of ways to pull out both fact and feelings data. For example:

Color Coding Feelings   To gather both facts and feelings, use colors to represent emotional states. For example:

- Blue = sad, mad, bad
- Red = challenged, stalled
- Green = satisfied, successful, energetic
- Yellow = cautious, confused
- Purple = fun, surprise, humor
- Salmon = fatigued, stressed

Color Coding Events   Use colors to represent types of events. For example:

- Yellow = technical or technology related
- Pink = people or team related
- Green = organization related

Color Coding Functions   Use colors to represent functions. For example:

- Blue = developers
- Pink = customers
- Green = QA and testing
- Yellow = technical writers

Color Coding Themes   If the team wants to focus on particular matters, use colors to identify events related to specific themes. For example:

- Yellow = team communication
- Blue = equipment usage
- Pink = relationships with customers
- Green = engineering practices

You can pick your own color scheme based on the cards and sticky notes available to you.

Functional Swim Lanes   Draw rows lengthwise along the backdrop for the timeline (assuming you aren't planning to post cards directly on the wall—then use ribbon or tape to demarcate the rows). Make a row for each department or function. That group will place their cards only in that swim lane.

In/Out Swim Lanes   Draw one line that divides the backdrop in half lengthwise. Use one half for cards for team events and the other half for participants who were involved in the project but not part of the core team.

On/Off   Use some special shape to represent the people on the project—stars or people-shaped cutouts are good. Ask people to represent when they started on the project by posting a star/people cutout on the timeline. Add a star or cutout for people who are no longer on the project or who aren't in the retrospective.

Materials and Preparation

Markers. Index cards or sticky notes. Drafting dots or some other movable tape that allows people to reposition event cards. Painter's tape or tacky stuff to paper the wall.

Backdrop. Cover a long wall with paper to serve as a backdrop. You can overlap flip chart pages or use roll paper. A stretch 6 feet long and 30 inches high is about right for a one-week iteration. For a longer project, you may need 30–60 feet long by 4–6 feet high.

Paper the wall before the retrospective starts.

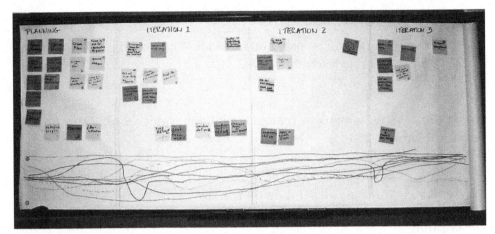

The team was just starting retrospectives and wanted to look back further than just one iteration.

Figure 7—A timeline for a retrospective that looked at three iterations

(For a release or project, prep the timeline with a few time markers such as project milestones, months, or seasons.)

Example

A timeline can display many levels of data about the iteration, release, or project. It can be a simple, chronological listing of events on white index cards. It can also be an extravaganza of data including color-coded themes, cards arranged high or low for meaning, swim lanes for different functional areas, dots to show positive and negative events, and a space at the bottom with a graph for the ongoing emotional ups and downs. It's easy to get carried away with the possible variations and ask teams to create a timeline with more data than they have time or mental energy to discuss.

When you have only an hour or so for the entire retrospective session, choose a timeline variation that will help to display just enough data. Include both facts and feelings, for sure, but no more than one kind of each. Consult the retrospective goal as a guide for what's most important this time. Keep it simple.

5.2 Activity: Triple Nickels

Use this to gather data or as part of the Decide What to Do phase in an iteration, release, or project retrospective.

Purpose

Generate ideas for actions or recommendations. Uncover important topics about the project history.

Time Needed

Thirty to sixty minutes, depending on the size of the group.

Description

Form small groups. In the groups, each person has five minutes to brainstorm and write down ideas individually. At the end of five minutes, each person passes the paper to the person on his or her right. That person has five minutes to write down ideas that build on the ideas already written on the paper. Repeat until the paper returns to the original writer.

Steps

1. Set up the activity by saying "In this activity, our goal is to generate as many ideas as we can about [topic]." Then explain the process (see the brief description earlier).

2. Divide the team into small groups, with no more than five in a group. Hand out paper for people to write on. Make sure each person has a pen or pencil. Remind people to write legibly so the next person can read the ideas.

3. Describe the process: In the first round, each person will have five minutes to write down ideas related to the topic. Aim for at least five ideas. In subsequent rounds, each person writes ideas that are sparked by the already written ideas or builds on them in some way.

4. Time the group. After five minutes, ring a chime and tell the group to pass the paper to the right.

5. Ask each person to read the ideas listed on the paper.

6. Debrief using these questions:

   • What did you notice while you wrote ideas?

   • What surprised you? What met your expectations? How?

- What is missing from these lists?

- What ideas and topics should we examine further?

Segue into the next activity where the team will use the ideas generated.

Materials and Preparation:

Paper. Pens or pencils.

Variations

If there are seven or fewer people in the group, don't divide into small groups; do the activity as whole group. Pass the paper only five times.

Examples

With a team of mostly reticent developers and one or two outspoken individuals, an activity like Triple Nickels can allow team members time to think privately yet participate in a process that develops whole-team understanding. It also prevents the few people who are comfortable talking in a group from dominating the discussion. In Triple Nickels, everyone gets the chance to contribute equally to developing the data set, and by the time the data is out, even the more reticent folks usually have something to say about what they wrote or read.

To help the five members of an internal business applications team gather data about their iteration, Aswaria, the retrospective leader, introduced the Triple Nickels activity. She divided the ten people on the team into two groups and passed out paper tablets and pens.

"I'll give you each five minutes to write down five important events that happened during our iteration. Record things you saw or heard during the past fifteen days. Write legibly; make sure someone else can read it."

At the end of five minutes, she said, "Now pass your papers to the right. Read what you get. You have five minutes to add detail to the items there or add new, related events."

The team kept passing the papers until each member received their original paper back to read. Some team members laughed at comments; others were shaking their heads. To maintain the theme of "fives," Aswaria debriefed with questions such as the following: "What five things stand out for you about what you've read?" "What five events produced the strongest reactions?" "What are the five most significant events?"

After they finished the discussion, she handed out sticky drafting dots and invited people to post the papers on an area of the wall that she had labeled "Iteration History."

5.3   Activity: Color Code Dots

Use this in conjunction with a timeline to gather data about feelings in a longer iteration, release, or project retrospective.

Purpose

Show how people experienced events on the timeline.

Time Needed

Five to twenty minutes.

Description

Team members use sticky dots to show events on the timeline where emotions ran high or low.

Steps

After all the events are on the timeline and the team has done a quick review, individuals use colored dots to show where their energy was high or low (see Figure 8, *A timeline with color-coded dots*, on page 58).

1. Set up the activity by saying "Now that we've seen the facts, let's see how it was to be doing this work."

2. Provide each individual with dots in two colors. Start with seven to ten dots per person but have more available. Explain which color indicates high energy and which indicates low energy.

3. Ask each person to use the dots to show where energy was high and where energy was stalled, flagging, or at low ebb.

Materials and Preparation

Sticky dots 1/2 to 3/4 inches in diameter in two colors.

Decide which color will indicate high energy and which will indicate low energy.

Variations

Instead of using dots to indicate high or low energy, use dots to indicate positive or negative events.

Examples

When you have limited time, this technique filters topics for discussion:

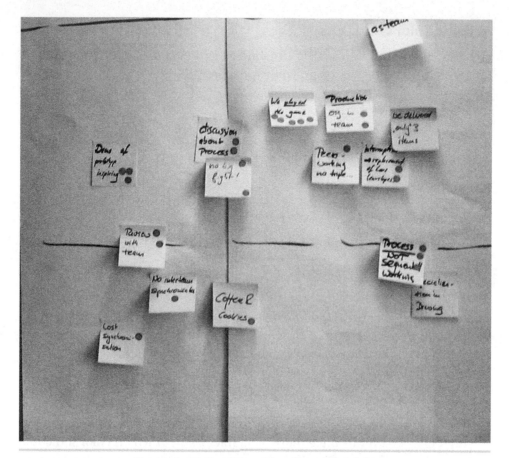

Figure 8—A timeline with color-coded dots

1. Investigate events that have many high energy or positive dots to learn what factors create that state.

2. Investigate low energy/negative events to learn what precipitated the event, and how the team resolved the situation.

3. Look at areas where there's a split (as with Carly's card in Chapter 1) to learn about the different perspectives.

5.4   Activity: Mad Sad Glad

Use this to gather data about feelings in an iteration, release, or project retrospective.

Purpose

Get the feeling facts out on the table.

Time needed

Twenty to thirty minutes, depending on the size of the group.

Description

Individuals use colored cards or sticky notes to describe times during the project where they were mad, sad, or glad.

Steps

Introduce the activity by saying "Let's look at how we were feeling during this iteration/release/project and discover whether we can track down some of the sources of both satisfying and dissatisfying times."

1. Draw attention to three posters labeled "Mad", "Sad", "Glad" and sample color-coded cards. Put out colored cards/sticky notes where everyone can reach them. Provide markers.

2. Describe the process, and give the time limit.

   "Take __ minutes to write down the times/events on this iteration/release /project where you were mad, sad, or glad. Write one event or incident per card. Write legibly."

3. Give notice when time is up, and invite people to post their cards on the appropriate poster. It's OK to add more cards as people remember more events.

4. Cluster the cards on each poster. Go to the first poster, pick one card, and read it. Then hold it next to another card and ask, "Are these cards about the same thing?" The group will tell you which other card it is like. Continue this until all the cards are clustered on each poster.

5. Ask the group to name each cluster. Use another card to write the title. Differentiate the title by drawing a box around the outer edge of the card or using a different color card.

6.   Debrief using these questions:

- What stands out for you as you look at these cards?

- What is unexpected about these cards? What was difficult about this task? What parts felt positive?

- What patterns do you see in the clusters? What do those patterns mean for us as a team?

- What does this suggest for us as next steps?

Materials and Preparation

Flip chart pages or some other surface for the posters. Three posters, labeled "Mad", "Sad", and "Glad". If your group has more than ten people, you may need two flip chart pages for each category poster.

Three colors of index cards or sticky notes. Make a sample card for each color so people can see the color-coding scheme. You can do this with one color of card, but the visual impact is greater with different colors.

Markers.

Variations

Rather than use the emotion words, make one poster labeled "Prouds" and another labeled "Sorries." Ask team members to write cards that represent events and interactions from the iteration that they feel proud about and events and interactions they feel sorry about.

Examples

This activity uncovers the emotional content of the retrospective. It's somehow easier to write down a "Mad" card about an event than say the words "I was angry when so-and-so happened."

Shift to "Prouds" and "Sorries" when there has been hurt feelings or conflicts. It's easier to write a card that indicates a person is sorry about an event than to articulate a direct apology or admit fault. But somehow writing the card communicates the intention of regret without assigning blame or admitting wrongdoing...and it works better for group relationships in the long run.

5.5   Activity: Locate Strengths

Use this to gather data about facts and feelings on longer iteration, release, and project retrospectives. Follow with the Identify Themes activity to generate insights.

Purpose

Identify strengths so the team can build on them in the next iteration. Provide balance when an iteration, release, or project hasn't gone well.

Time Needed

Fifteen to forty minutes for the Locate Strengths activity, depending on the number of questions in the interview. Allow twenty to forty more to identify themes. The total for the two activities is thirty to ninety minutes.

Description

Team members interview each other about high points on the project. The goal is to understand the sources and circumstances that created those high point (*Appreciative Inquiry: Change at the Speed of Imagination* [WM01]).

Steps

Introduce the activity by saying "We learn by asking questions. We learn the most about the things we ask the most questions about. Since we want to learn about having successful iterations (release/projects), let's take time to ask each other questions about high points."

1. Form pairs. If it's possible, pair people who don't know each other's job well or don't work together often. If there's an odd number, have one trio. Hand out the interview questions.

2. Explain the interview process:

    - Stay curious.

    - Give the speaker your full attention.

    - Take notes to remember key points.

    - Listen for stories and quotes to share.

    - This isn't a conversation—the interviewer asks questions and listens without interjecting his or her own story.

When the first interview is finished, switch roles.

3. Have the pairs choose who will interview first. Monitor the time, and ring a chime or make an announcement when half the time has elapsed. Say, "If you haven't started your second interview, start it soon."

4. At the end of the interviews, segue to the Identify Themes activity.

Materials and Preparation

Prepare questions ahead of time, and make enough copies for each person to have one.

Questions follow this format:

- Ask about what attracted the person to his or her profession or to the company.
- Ask about a high point on the iteration/release/project where the person was at his or her best.
- Ask what made it a high point.
- Ask who else was present and what the circumstances were.
- Ask about wishes for future projects.

Examples

Here's an example of an interview:

"Tell me about what attracted you to this company."

"In every release (iteration or project), there are high points when things just click. Think back over our last release. (Pause.) Tell me a story about one of your highlight moments."

"What were the circumstances?"

"Who else contributed?"

"If you had three wishes to make our next [iteration, release, project] better, what would they be?"

A short interview like this one will take about fifteen minutes per person. Adding more questions adds to the interview time. If you do add questions, follow the same general outline, probing for more detail about the high point situation.

This is a good activity when people are feeling downtrodden. It helps them remember that even dismal iterations have good moments. Focusing on high points helps people become conscious about re-creating the circumstances behind them. The problems will still come out, but they come out with less depression and rancor.

5.6   Activity: Satisfaction Histogram

Use this activity to set the stage and/or gather data in an iteration retrospective.

Purpose

Highlight how satisfied team members are with a focus area. Provide a visual picture of current status in a particular area to help the team have deeper discussions and analysis. Acknowledge differences in perspective among team members.

Time needed

Five to ten minutes.

Description

Team members use a histogram to gauge individual and group satisfaction with practices and process.

Steps

1. Introduce the activity by saying "Today we'll create a baseline measure of our level of satisfaction with the way we work together. We can repeat this activity in future iteration retrospectives to track our progress."

2. Show the flip charts to the team, read the definitions, and hand out index cards or other identical small slips of paper, one to each team member.

   "Please write a number on your card that tells your level of satisfaction on the team right now. Then fold the card, and put it in a pile here."

3. Stir the pile of cards, and ask for a volunteer to color in the graph as you read them. Read the number on each card. Wait for the tally before going on to the next.

4. Read the results from the graph. Ask for comments.

   You may comment on the data yourself: "It seems we have three people who are very satisfied on this team and two who aren't, and the rest of us are somewhere in the middle. As we continue with our retrospective, we can keep these results in mind as we choose experiments for the next iteration. We'll check back to remeasure in a few iterations."

Materials and Preparation

Prepare two flip charts. On one flip chart write numbers 1 through 5 in descending order with the following definitions, or your own variations (see Figure 9, *Post the definitions for the satisfaction rating*, on page 66). On the other flip chart, write numbers one through five down the left margin with rows of boxes to fill in as you tally the votes (see Figure 10, *Satisfaction histogram*, on page 67).

Variations

Process is just one possibility for a satisfaction histogram. Some other possibilities are quality of the product, interactions outside the team, or engineering practices.

Where We're At Variation   Use this variation to set the stage for a retrospective. Change the five definitions to ask about the overall level of satisfaction with the iteration or ask about team member's satisfaction with how the day has started.

For example:

- "5 = The way this day has started, it may be the best day of my life. I'm extremely satisfied."

- "4 = I've had a good start to the day. I'm quite satisfied with it so far."

- "3 = This day has started okay. I'm moderately satisfied with it."

- "2 = This day started slightly worse than most days. I'm only a little satisfied with it."

- "1 = I got up on the wrong side of the bed and nothing has gone right yet. I am not satisfied with how the day has started."

Examples

This activity is a quick and painless way to uncover emotional data without the *F* word. It can be interesting to use two histograms on different factors, such as satisfaction with the product and satisfaction with process. One group we worked with was highly satisfied with their process but not satisfied with the resulting product. Another team was the opposite: satisfied with the product but unsatisfied with the way they achieved a good result with the product.

In the first case, team members had been hiding their dissatisfaction with the product to avoid hurting feelings. After seeing the histogram, the team

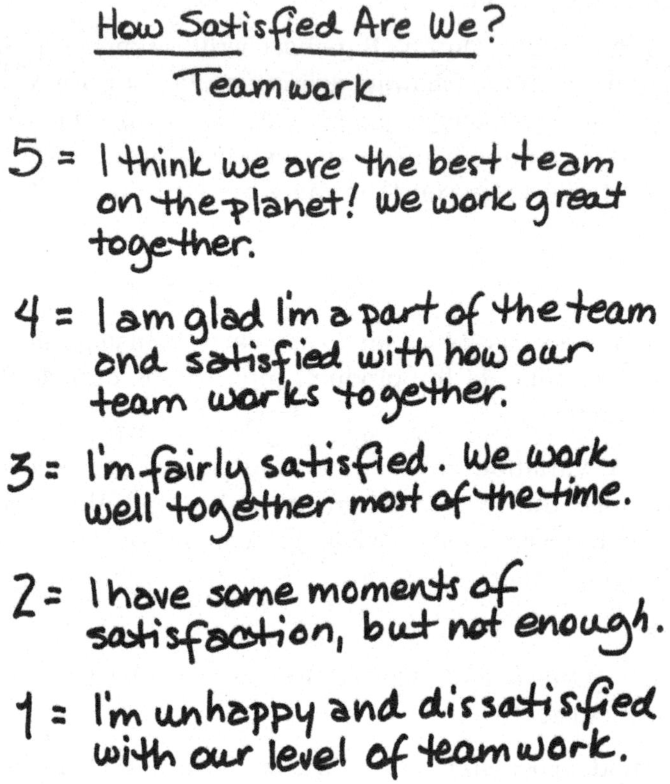

How Satisfied Are We?

Teamwork

5 = I think we are the best team on the planet! we work great together.

4 = I am glad I'm a part of the team and satisfied with how our team works together.

3 = I'm fairly satisfied. We work well together most of the time.

2 = I have some moments of satisfaction, but not enough.

1 = I'm unhappy and dissatisfied with our level of teamwork.

Figure 9—Post the definitions for the satisfaction rating

had frank discussions about how they avoided conflict. Over the next few iterations, they were more direct with each other. When the team rechecked their satisfaction two months later, they were more satisfied on both measures.

The second team (satisfied with product, dissatisfied with process) examined their engineering practices and how they contributed to defects and extra work. They identified experiments to improve engineering practices.

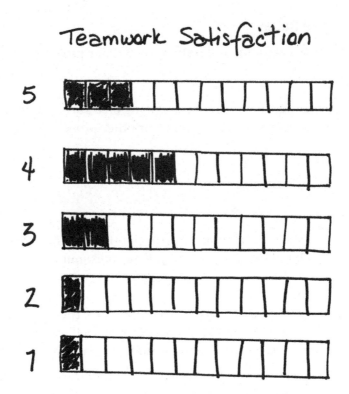

The data shown on this histogram creates an opportunity for the team to discuss different perceptions of how well they are working together.

Figure 10—Satisfaction histogram

5.7 Activity: Team Radar

Use this to gather data in an iteration, release, or project retrospective.

Purpose

Help the team gauge how well they are doing on a variety of measures, such as, engineering practices, team values, or other processes.

Time Needed

Fifteen to twenty minutes.

Description

Team members track individual and group ratings for specific factors about process or development practices they want to examine.

Steps

1. Introduce the activity by saying "We agreed on these [fill in the factors] as important to our work. Let's assess how well we are doing, using a scale of 0–10. Zero means not at all, and 10 means as much as possible."

2. Post the flip chart with the blank radar graph. Ask each team member to approach the chart and place a dot or some other mark that shows their rating for each factor.

3. Lead a short discussion about how the factors affect the work of the team. Consider asking questions such as the following:

    • Where do you see us following these [fill in factors]?
    • Where do you not see us following these [fill in the factors]?

   Use the short discussion as a segue to generating insights.

4. Save the completed flip chart graph. Run the activity again two or three iterations later. Compare the two charts as a progress measure.

Materials and Preparation

Flip chart or white board. Markers.

If you know ahead of time what the team will measure using the radar chart, draw the spokes and label them ahead of time (See Figure 11, *Team radar*, on page 69). If the team will brainstorm the measures during the retrospective, draw the radar chart during the retrospective.

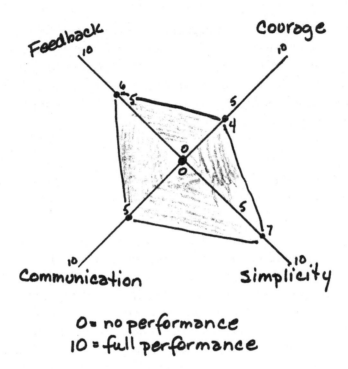

This team used the Group Average Radar to gauge how much they were following their team values.

Figure 11—Team radar

Variations

You can use this activity to measure many different factors, such as, engineering practices, team values, working agreements, methods, and so forth.

Group Average Radar   This variation is an ongoing measure of progress on a particular measure. Use the radar chart but instead of collecting individual responses, calculate the group average for each measure.

Hand each team member a set of colored cards, one for each factor measured. Ask each person to rate each factor from 0–10 and hand the card to you.

Shuffle the cards (within colors) as you receive them so it's not clear which card came from a particular team member.

Recruit a team member to help with calculating averages. Post the averages on the radar arms. Connect the dots, and color in the area under the line (optional).

Prepare a set of index cards in different colors for each team member. Write the name of one measure on all the cards of a single color. So if you are measuring team values (as in Figure 11, *Team radar*, on page 69), all the green cards would have "Communication" written on one side, all the blue cards would have "Courage", and so on. Each team member receives a set of cards that includes each factor measured.

Examples

Team Radar is a subjective measure that's intended to generate discussion. This is especially useful when you suspect there's no common definition or criteria to measure against.

For example, one team used a radar to examine how team members perceived their use of a number of engineering practices, including refactoring. One team member rated their refactoring 8; another rated it at 3. During the discussion that followed, it became clear that each had different ideas on when to refactor. Further, the team member who rated her refactoring low was upset with the team member who rated his refactoring high because he was "slacking off by not refactoring enough." By the end of the retrospective, the team arrived at a common definition. Over the next few iterations, the team was more consistent in when they refactored, and resentment faded.

5.8   Activity: Like to Like

Use to gather data during an iteration, release, or project retrospecti

Purpose

Help team members recall their experiences during the iteration (release or project), and hear that others may have perceived it differently.

Time Needed

Thirty to forty minutes.

Description

Team members take turns judging which events or factors about their itcration are the best fits for quality cards. As the cards are evaluated, team members learn about each other's perspective on the same events or conditions.

Steps

1. Ask each team member to write at least nine index cards for playing the Like to Like game: three or more cards with things to stop doing three or more cards with things to keep doing and three or more things to start doing. While team members are writing, shuffle the deck of colored "quality" cards and lay the pile face down on a table.

2. When the game cards are ready, invite the team to stand around the table. Choose one person to start as "judge." The "judge" turns over a "quality" card from the pile and puts it face up on the table. All other team members look in their game cards for the one that most closely matches the "quality" card and place their cards face down. The last card down is disqualified and returns to its owner's hand. This keeps the game moving.

3. The "judge" stirs the players' cards, turns them over one at a time, and reads them. He or she chooses the card that makes the best match with the "quality" card. The author of that card wins the "quality" card.

4. The role of "judge" passes left to the next person, and another "quality" card is turned over. After six to nine rounds (or whenever everyone runs out of cards), the game ends. The person with the most "quality" cards wins.

5. Debrief the activity with the four-step method.

Materials and Preparation

Buy or borrow an Apples to Apples game, and play it with your friends or family to get the idea of Like to Like.

Blank index cards for the participants (at least nine for every person).

Prepare a set of approximately twenty "quality" cards on yellow (or other color) index cards. Write one word on each card. These cards have the words *Fun, On Time, Clear, Meaningful, Affordable, Integrated, Educational, Talented, Smooth, Cool, Speedy, Collaborative, Awesome, Trustworthy, Dangerous, Frustrating, Creepy, Nasty* or others. Include some "serious" words like *on time*, and some "fun" words like *cool* or *nasty*. It keeps the game less predictable, more insightful and more enjoyable.

Variations

For XP projects, combine this game with the Industrial Logic[1] XP cards. Deal the XP cards, and let people play them instead of writing their own cards, in the sense of "The way we did X embodies this quality" (so a team member might play "Planning Game" on "Frustrating" if that week's session went poorly, but wouldn't play "Integrations take too long" if they didn't.)

Example

A storage solutions software team played the *Like to Like* game in their release retrospective. Team members discovered that game cards about communication and lab procedures were consistently matched with undesirable quality cards. As the "judges" considered their choices and team member advocated for game cards, they told stories about how decisions got made and communicated.

In planning action items for the next release, team members listed their top three priorities: improve communication with the core team about expectations, increase contact with internal customers, and bring new team members up to speed more quickly. They also made a recommendation to their managers to start new distributed project teams with an initial face-to-face meeting.

---

1.   http://www.industriallogic.com

CHAPTER 6

Activities to Generate Insights

Generating insights makes time for the team to evaluate their data and make meaningful information from it. These activities help the team interpret the data, analyze it, generate insights, and uncover the implications for change.

6.1 Activity: Brainstorming/Filtering

Use this to generate insights in an iteration, release, or project retrospective.

Purpose

Generate a large number of ideas and filter them against a defined set of criteria.

Time Needed

Forty to sixty minutes.

Description

Team members generate ideas using traditional brainstorming, then test whether each idea is applicable to the current situation.

Steps

1. Introduce the activity by saying "Because we need to push beyond our usual thinking, we're going to spend the next chunk of time brainstorming. Once we've generated new approaches, we'll filter the ideas to find the ones that fit best for our situation."

2. Describe the guidelines for brainstorming (Figure 12, *Typical guidelines for brainstorming*, on page 75).

    Challenge the group to come up with fifty ideas, and set the time limit, usually ten to fifteen minutes.

3. Brainstorm using one of three methods:

    * Brainstorming Method 1: Free-for-all. People call out ideas at random.

    * Brainstorming Method 2: Round-robin. Pass a "talking token" around the circle. Only the person holding the talking token can talk. It's OK to pass when your turn comes.

    * Brainstorming Method 3: Give people five to seven minutes to silently and individually generate and write down ideas. When the time is up, use Brainstorming Method 1 or 2.

    * Monitor time, and call when the time has run out.

4. Ask the group what filters they should apply to the ideas. Accept four to eight suggestions, discuss, and then vote using a show of hands on

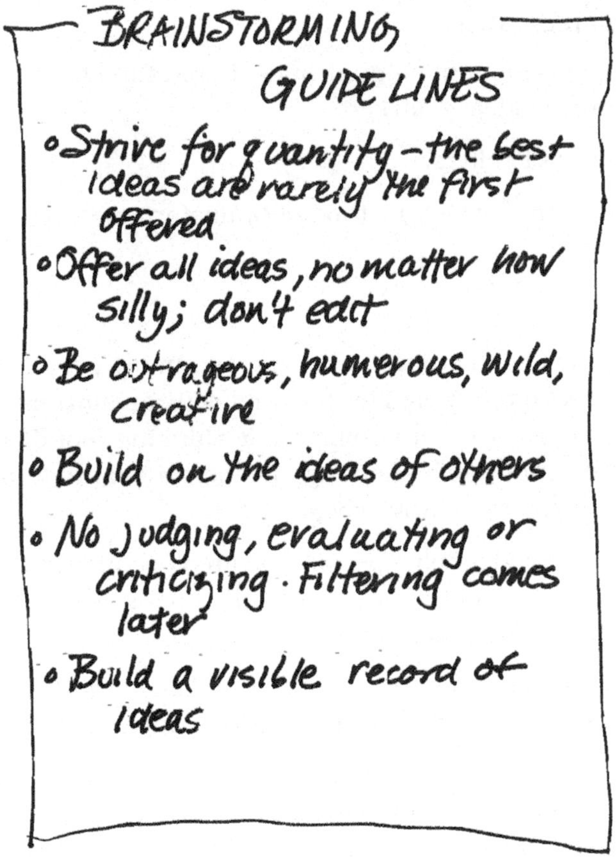

BRAINSTORMING
GUIDELINES
○ Strive for quantity — the best
   ideas are rarely the first
   offered
○ Offer all ideas, no matter how
   silly; don't edit
○ Be outrageous, humerous, wild,
   creative
○ Build on the ideas of others
○ No judging, evaluating or
   criticizing. Filtering comes
   later
○ Build a visible record of
   ideas

Figure 12—Typical guidelines for brainstorming

the top four. Write the four selected filters on a separate flip chart page or on the white board.

5. Apply the filters one at a time to the ideas on the brainstorm lists. Cross out items that don't pass the filters. Mark ideas that pass each filter. Use a different color for each filter.

6. Look for ideas that pass all four filters.

7. Ask for comments on the ideas. Ask the group which ideas they want to carry forward. Ask whether anyone feels strongly about taking responsibility for any of the ideas. If someone feels strongly, it's a good bet to carry forward. Otherwise, use the simple majority vote.

8. Carry the selected ideas into the next phase, Decide What to Do.

Materials and Preparation

Flip chart with brainstorming guidelines. Blank flip chart pages or white board for capturing ideas. Markers.

Examples of possible filters.

Choose ahead of time which method of brainstorming will work best with your team.

Examples

Brainstorming has been around for years, and many people have heard of it. The problem with traditional brainstorming (Brainstorming Method 1) is that it favors people who are comfortable thinking aloud. It also favors people who are comfortable shouting out their thoughts in a group. That leaves out many smart, creative people.

Brainstorming Method 2 helps people who aren't comfortable shouting out in a group participate and leaves an escape (saying "pass") to people who haven't thought of anything... yet.

Brainstorming Method 3 helps people who need time to gather their thoughts (like Esther) time to do that, and then they're ready to participate in Brainstorming Method 1 or 2.

A fourth variation on the activity is to take the ideas generated in Brainstorming Method 3 and write them on cards. After Brainstorming Method 3, people write their ideas on cards and then hand them to the retrospective leader, who posts them and reads them. Even the quietest person can write his or her idea on a card for someone else to read.

6.2 Activity: Force Field Analysis

Use this in conjunction with an activity that suggests possible changes while generating insights for a release or project retrospective. Use this as part of a planning exercise while deciding what to do.

Purpose

To examine what factors in the organization will support a proposed change and which will inhibit the change.

Time Needed

Forty-five to sixty minutes depending on the complexity of the issue and the size of the group.

Description

The team defines a desired state they want to achieve. Small groups work to identify the factors that could either restrain or drive the change they want. The factors are listed on a poster; then the group assesses the strength of each supporting factor relative to the other supporting factors and repeats the process for inhibiting factors. The team discusses which factors they can influence—either by increasing the strength of a supporting factor or by reducing the strength of an inhibiting factor.

Steps

1. Introduce the activity by saying "If we want this change to succeed, we need to understand more about the factors that will support or inhibit the change."

2. Describe the process.

   Break into small groups (no more than four).

   "Each group works for __ minutes to identify factors that will drive or support the change."

   "We'll do a round-robin report of what you discover and post the results. Then we'll repeat the process for restraining or inhibiting factors."

   "After we've listed both sets of factors, we'll assess their relative strength and discuss what course of action would be most helpful for implementing the change we want."

3. Monitor time and the activity level.

While the groups are working, prepare a flip chart like the one pictured in Figure 13, *Force Field analysis*, on page 79 (but don't fill in the factors yet).

4. When the group is finished with the first task (identifying supporting or driving factors) collect the information the small groups have generated in round-robin fashion, asking for one factor at a time. There's no need to repeat duplicates; collect only the unique factors.

5. Repeat for restraining or inhibiting factors.

6. Bring the whole group back together, and examine each factor and gauge its strength relative to the other factors. Draw a line toward the center arrow indicating relative strength. Do this first for driving and then for restraining factors.

7. Examine the factors for most effective actions:

   • Ask the group how they can strengthen driving factors or mitigate restraining factors.

   • Ask the group whether enhancing driving factors or reducing restraining factors is more likely to achieve the desired state.

Materials and Preparation

Flip chart paper or a white board. Markers.

Identify an issue to analyze, perhaps from a list of proposed improvements or another generating insights activity, such as Five Whys or Fishbone.

Example

Force Field Analysis is another tool to ensure that the changes your team identifies in their retrospective actually happen. Combine creating the Force Field Analysis graph with a discussion of influence and control. What can the team directly control to make a change? What can't they control, and where are their points of influence in the situation? Most teams have more ability to influence conditions than they realize; however, a team needs to think about the most effective ways and times to use their influence. Force Field Analysis can help them discern points of greatest leverage and, sometimes, help them see that changing a situation may require more effort than the outcome they desire will be worth. Other times, they may see the forces allied against them and decide to tackle the issue anyway.

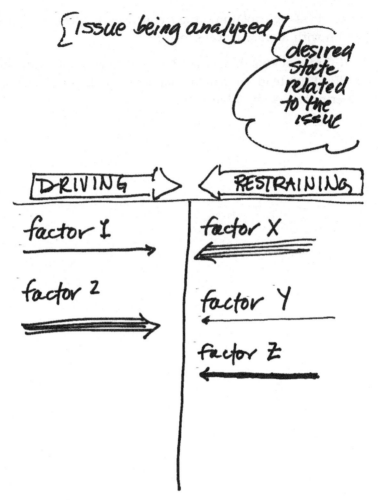

Force Field analysis helps the team look at factors affecting a proposed change.

Figure 13—Force Field analysis

One team came into their retrospective wanting to change the way they interacted with the product owner. They were dissatisfied with the limited contact and communication that occurred during the iteration. The product owner answered questions, but only after several days had passed.

Before they analyzed the situation by drawing a Force Field Analysis poster, they understood that the product owner's travel schedule and times of availability were outside their control. Afterward, they also saw they could exert influence best by explaining their concerns to the VP of Marketing, another person with a crazy travel schedule.

They decided that tracking down the VP would take more team effort than they could afford. Instead, they made plans to get the most out of the few product owner contacts available to them.

6.3 Activity: Five Whys

Use this to generate insights in an iteration, release, or project retrospective.

Purpose

Discover underlying conditions that contribute to an issue.

Time Needed

Fifteen to twenty minutes.

Description

Team members work in pairs or small groups to look at issues. They ask "Why?" times to get beyond habitual thinking.

Steps

Introduce the activity by saying "Now that we know what's happened, let's look at why it happened."

1. Review the issues and themes that the team has already identified.

2. Divide the team into pairs or small groups (no more than four to a group). And explain the process.

   "One person asks the other(s) why an event or problem occurred."

   "In response to the answer, the questioner asks why that happened."

   "Record the responses that come out of the fourth or fifth 'Why?'"

3. Monitor the time, and ring a chime or otherwise announce when the time is up.

4. Have the groups report what they discovered.

5. Use this information as input into the next phase, Decide What to Do.

Materials and Preparation

Use this in conjunction with an activity that generates themes or a list of potential problems, for example Patterns and Shifts.

Examples

Here's an example. Say the issue is that the iteration review meeting never starts on time.

Q1: Why did we start our review meeting late on Thursday?

A: The room wasn't available.

Q2: Why wasn't the room available?

A: We forgot to put it on the meeting schedule.

Q3: Why did we forget to put it on the meeting schedule?

A: Charlie was out sick, and he always schedules the room.

Q4: Why does just Charlie schedule the room?

A: Because we didn't think it would matter.

Q5: Why didn't we think having the room scheduled mattered?

A: We didn't understand how much of our time it would waste. But we understand now. We could add it to our review preparation checklist.

6.4 Activity: Fishbone

Use this activity to generate insights in a longer iteration, release, or project retrospective.

Purpose

Look past symptoms to identify root causes related to an issue. Look for reasons behind problems and breakdowns.

Time Needed

Thirty to sixty minutes.

Description

The team identifies factors that are causing or affecting a problem situation and then looks for the most likely causes. After they've identified the most likely causes, they look for ways they can make changes or influence those factors.

Steps

1. Draw a fishbone diagram (see Figure 14, *Fishbone*, on page 85) and write the problem or issue at the fish's head. Include the five W's—What, Who, When, Where, and Why. Label the "bones" of the fish with categories.

   Typical categories are as follows:

   - Methods, Machines, Materials, Staffing (which was formerly known as Manpower)
   - Place, Procedure, People, Policies
   - Surroundings, Suppliers, Systems, Skills

   You can use these in any combination, or the team can identify their own categories.

2. Brainstorm factors within each category. Prompt by asking "What are the [fill in a category name here] issues causing or affecting [fill in the problem here.]" Repeat this for each category. Write the issues along the bones, or have people write them on small sticky notes and stick them to the fishbone diagram.

3. Continue asking "Why is this happening?"

   Add more branches off the bones as needed.

   Stop when the causes are outside the team's control or influence.

4. Look for items that appear in more than one category. These may be the most likely causes. Engage the group in looking for areas where they can make a difference.

Use the results in the next phase, Decide What to Do.

Materials and Preparation

Markers, sticky notes.

Define the problem statement. Include the five W's— What, Who, When, Where, and Why—to the extent they are known. Draw the fishbone diagram on a flip or white board. Make a list of the sample categories.

Examples

Use a Fishbone activity to dig into the root causes of a problem, but don't stop there. A fully branched and labeled diagram is not a deliverable of the retrospective.

If you suspect that a lot of what will come up in the retrospective may be due to issues outside the team's control, digging into all the problem sources may drain the team's energy. Choose a different method.

When the issues are more local to the team and under their direct control, the team may be energized by tackling the fishbones.

For example, during a two-week iteration, the build broke five times. The retrospective leader knew the team was frustrated by it, and the broken build would be a prominent topic in the retrospective. He introduced the Fishbone activity with bones labeled "Skills", "Systems", "Surroundings", and "Staffing".

Two or three team members worked in small groups to focus on writing sticky notes for each bone. They covered the "fish" with scales of notes.

When they stepped back to read the notes, they saw two root causes—inexperienced team members working alone (showed up in both Skills and Staffing) and writing new code while waiting for the build to compile (showed up in both Systems and Surroundings). Everyone immediately agreed on a commitment to mentor and pair with newer team members. They identified the second cause as needing more attention and decided to include it as a topic of action planning.

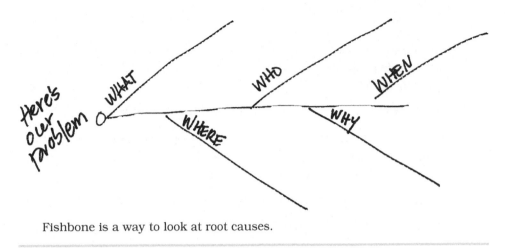

Fishbone is a way to look at root causes.

Figure 14—Fishbone

6.5 Activity: Patterns and Shifts

Use this in conjunction with a visual data-gathering activity (e.g., Timeline or Mad, Sad, Glad) to generate insights in an iteration, release, or project retrospective.

Purpose

Look for links and connection between facts and feelings. Analyze the data about the iteration/release/project. Guide the group in recognizing and naming patterns that contribute to current issues.

Time Needed

Fifteen to sixty minutes, depending on the size of the group and the amount of data.

Description

After gathering data, facilitate a discussion to analyze the data, looking for patterns of events, behaviors, or feelings. Also look for times when there has been a shift; for example, everything was going smoothly, and then the energy dropped. Capture insights on flip charts or, if you're using a timeline, right on the timeline.

Steps

1. Introduce the activity by saying "Now that we've created a picture of our iteration/release project, let's see what patterns and information we can find in our data."

2. Invite the group to examine the display, if they haven't already.

3. Focus on section at a time, and ask the group what they notice about the data. Write notes about what they say on the display or on a separate flip chart. Go through section by section.

4. Now look at the entire display. Ask the group:

    • Where do you see connections and links between events?

    • Where do you see a pattern? What would you name that pattern?

    • Where do shifts occur? What would you name the shifts?

    Again, make notes on the display or on a separate flip chart.

5. Review the patterns and shifts. Ask the group the following questions:

    • How do these patterns contribute to our current issues?

    • What do these shifts tell us about our current issues?

6. Ask which ones are most important to address in the next phase of the retrospective, Decide What to Do.

Materials and Preparation

Markers and flip chart paper or cards.

Use this after a visual data gathering exercise such as Timeline or Mad, Sad, Glad.

6.6   Activity: Prioritize with Dots

Use this in the Generate Insights or Decide What to Do phase in an iteration release or project retrospective.

Purpose

To gauge how the group prioritizes a long list of candidate changes, proposals, and so forth.

Time Needed

Five to twenty minutes depending on the number of options and the size of the group.

Description

Team members prioritize the top issues, ideas, or proposals.

Steps

Introduce the activity by saying "We have a great list; we can't pursue all of the items, so let's see what the group views as the top priorities."

1. Give each team member ten 1/2" or 3/4" colored sticky dots. Post a legend allocating the dots as follows:

    - #1 priority receives four dots.

    - #2 priority receives three dots.

    - #3 priority receives two dots.

    - #4 priority receives one dot.

    Read the dot allocation scheme. Review the items under consideration.

2. Allow a few minutes for people to place their dots next to the items under consideration (see Figure 15, *Prioritizing with dots*, on page 89).

3. Count the number of dot on each item. Write the number next to the item.

4. When there are clear winners, ask the group whether they want to proceed with these items.

    When there's a tie at the top (four or more items receive the same number of dots) and it's not feasible to pursue all the top issues, ask the group to discuss why they see each one as a top priority, and then revote (preferably with a different colored dots).

Variations

Rather than provide ten dots per person with an allocation scheme, give each team member a number of dots roughly equal to 1/3 to 1/2 the total number of items. Team members can allocate their dots as they choose—all dots on one item, one dot per item, or anything in between.

To constrain the selection, offer fewer dots.

Materials and Preparation

Sticky dots—1/2"–3/4" in diameter. Have two colors in case you need to revote.

You can have people put check marks by the items, but dots are more fun and easier to count.

Example

Dot voting is not scientific. Don't try to make it scientific. It's a way to winnow down a long list of possibilities.

We've found that we get very different results depending on how we phrase a question. Here are some variations to consider:

- Which is the most important to work on?

- Which will have the greatest impact?

- Which do you want to work on most?

If no one wants to work on the "most important" or "greatest impact" items, it's a moot point. People can think an item is important and still not want to work on it. Go with the energy. You want action and decisions the group will support. The best choice is the one the team will do something about.

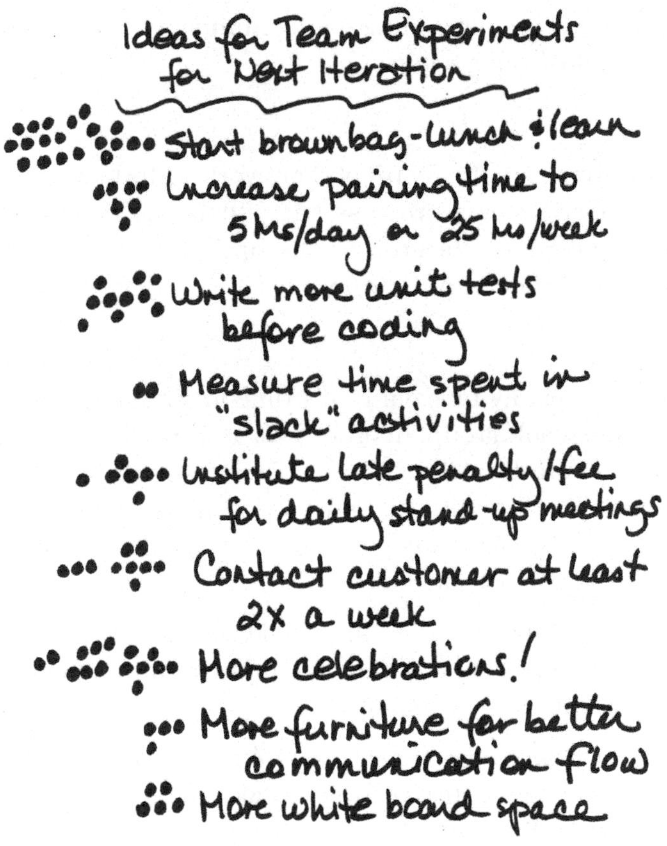

Ideas for Team Experiments
for Next Iteration

Start brownbag-lunch & learn

Increase pairing time to
5 hrs/day or 25 hrs/week

Write more unit tests
before coding

Measure time spent in
"slack" activities

Institute late penalty/fee
for daily stand-up meetings

Contact customer at least
2× a week

More celebrations!

More furniture for better
communication flow

More white board space

Prioritizing with dots helps a group winnow down a long list of items.

Figure 15—Prioritizing with dots

6.7 Activity: Report Out with Synthesis

Use this in conjunction with a small group analysis activity to generate insights in an iteration, release, or project retrospective.

Purpose

Share thinking and ideas from small groups with the whole group. Find common threads, and look for ideas that energize the whole group.

Time Needed

Twenty to sixty minutes, depending on the number of small groups and the amount of time allowed for reports.

Description

Each small group shares the result of their work with the whole group. The retrospective leader keeps a progress bar to help the reporter stay within time. After the final report, the group looks for common threads and themes and identifies those they want to work on.

Steps

1. Introduce the activity by saying "It's time for the teams to report their findings to the whole group. In order to hear from everyone, we can allow each group n minutes. I'll help you stay on track by keeping a progress bar. I'll mark off each minute, and when you see $n-1$ bars, you'll know it's time to wrap up. We'll have n minutes for questions after each report. I'll keep a progress bar for that, too."

2. Time carefully. Monitor time, and make a bar for each minute that passes. If someone is going over, at n minutes announce, "Time is up. Please take a minute to conclude."

3. After the last group report, ask the group to review any flip chart, or think back over what they've heard. Ask for common threads. Write those ideas on a flip chart.

4. After the group has identified common threads, ask these questions:

    • Which ideas to you have energy to tackle?

    • What is it about those items that you have energy for?

    • Which ideas have the greatest chance of success?

    • What's your overall impression of these ideas?

    • Which ideas do you want to take on in the next iteration?

5. Take the prioritized ideas into the next phase, Decide What to Do.

Materials and Preparation

Flip chart page prepared to track progress bars for all groups (see Figure 16, *Progress bar*, on page 92). A marker, but *not* a black marker. People have too many bad associations with having a black mark next to their name or team name. This is one time we like to use dark pink or orange markers.

Examples

Some people do go on. We've found that helping people monitor their own time helps them stay on track, stay on point, and finish on time. Actually, when people know they'll be timed, they tend to organize their thoughts more and often say what they need to say with time left over.

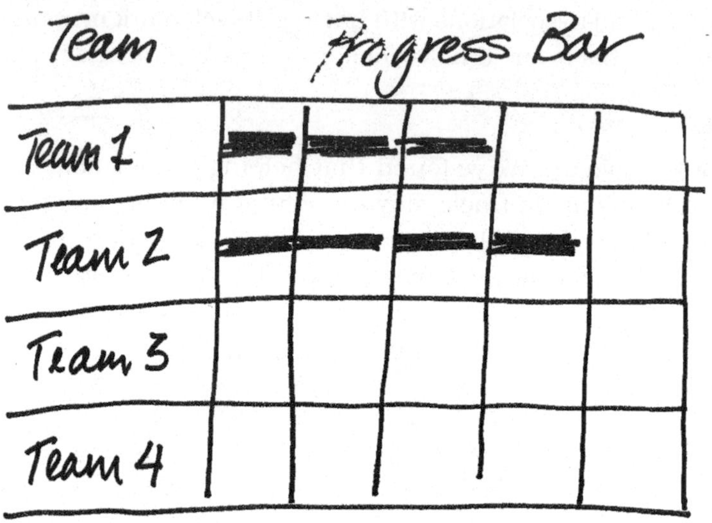

A visible progress bar helps the person reporting keep it brief.

Figure 16—Progress bar

6.8 Activity: Identify Themes

Use this after locating strengths to generate insights in a longer iteration, release, or project retrospective.

Purpose

Find common threads from Locate Strengths interviews. Discern compelling ideas for experiments, changes, and recommendations.

Time needed

One to two hours.

Description

After Locate Strengths interviews, the interview pairs form groups and report what each learned as they interviewed the other person. As they report the high points, team members listen for common themes and compelling ideas. After the identifying themes, the group clusters all the cards. Small groups self-select to further define the ideas contained in the cluster.

Steps

1. After interviews are complete, put two or three interview pairs together to form a group of four or six. Keep interview pairs together.

2. Explain the process.

   "Each interviewer will report on what he or she heard during the interview. Don't worry about reporting the interview verbatim or covering all the points. Report on memorable themes, stories, and quotes heard in the interview."

   "After all the stories have been recounted, discuss the common themes that came up in more than one interview. Make a note of compelling ideas—even if they came up in only one report."

   "Write each idea on a large index card. Write legibly so others can read the card. One idea per card."

3. Each group reports on the themes they heard and posts their cards on a wall or spreads them out on the floor.

4. After all the groups have reported, the entire group sorts the cards in like clusters.

5. Ask people to select a cluster that they want to work on refining. It's OK if no one chooses some of the clusters.

6. Small groups work on further defining steps for building on the strength themes.

7. Groups report on their work, which will become candidates for further planning, experiments, and recommendations in the Decide What to Do phase.

Materials and Preparation

This activity follows the Locate Strengths interview activity.

Large index cards and markers. Repositionable tape or tacky stuff to do the sorting on the wall.

Examples

A while back, we worked with a large group who were looking at how to make changes in their organization. One part of the group insisted that the best approach was to list all the problems and then identify solutions. Rather than fight with them, we let them go their way and worked with the rest of the group using interviews and identifying themes.

After two hours, the problem-solving group was drained, depressed, and ready to give up the whole enterprise.

Our group was energized and hopeful.

Coincidence? You decide.

6.9   Activity: Learning Matrix

Use this to generate insights in an iteration retrospective.

Purpose

Help team members find what's significant in their data.

Time Needed

Twenty to twenty-five minutes.

Description

Team members look at four perspectives on their data to brainstorm a list of issues quickly.

Steps

1. After discussing the data, show the flip chart (see Figure 17, *Learning matrix*, on page 97). Tell the team they can fill out the quarters in any order as thoughts come to them.

2. As team members think of ideas to add to the chart, write them in the corresponding section. Stick to writing the words they use as closely as possible. If you need to shorten a statement, ask the team member to paraphrase, "Could you please say that again using fewer words, so I can get it on the chart?"

   Variation: Give every team member a stack of sticky notes to write their ideas, one per sticky note. Each team member puts his or her notes in the appropriate quarter of the chart. The retrospective leader reads all the notes and sorts them into natural clusters.

3. When the flow of ideas slows down, review the comments on the chart. Ask the group, "Is there anything missing from this list? What haven't we written down that will be important to going forward?" Lead a brief discussion, and make additions, if needed.

4. Hand out strips of six to ten dots. "Place your dots to vote for the items that you believe have the highest priority to get attention during the next iteration." (Or you can use the honor system and give each person a marker to make a limited number of check marks.)

5. Use the prioritized list as an outcome to segue into your Decide What to Do phase.

Materials and Preparation

Prepare a flip chart (see Figure 17, *Learning matrix*, on page 97) in quarters with icons for the four sections: a "smiley" for, what did we do well that we want to continue? a "frowny" for, what would we like to change? a "light bulb" for, what new ideas have come up? and a "bouquet" for, who do we want to appreciate?

Prepare strips of dots, six to ten, depending on what's easy to cut from the page. (Variation: Substitute other kinds of stickers for dots. Children's stores, stationery, scrapbooking, and office-supply stores carry a variety of styles and kinds.)

Examples

We introduce the Learning Matrix whenever we are pressed for time to generate insights. This can happen in sixty to ninety-minute retrospectives where the data gathering turns into a longer discussion than we expected. We still want a rich discussion, but we have to get it as efficiently as possible.

The lines demarcating the four quadrants of the poster tend to serve as natural "brakes" on the discussion for each section. People fill up all the quadrants and stop offering ideas when they get to the lines or the bottom of the flip chart sheet. Then, ask, "What one additional idea about [what went well] should we include?" and write it around the title area. This ensures that the best ideas are not lost and you can stick to the timebox.

In the same way, when we are short of time, we use the Learning Matrix to gather feedback on the retrospective in the Close the Retrospective phase. Focus the four quadrants on the team's experiences during the retrospective—what went well, what do we want to do differently, new ideas, and appreciations.

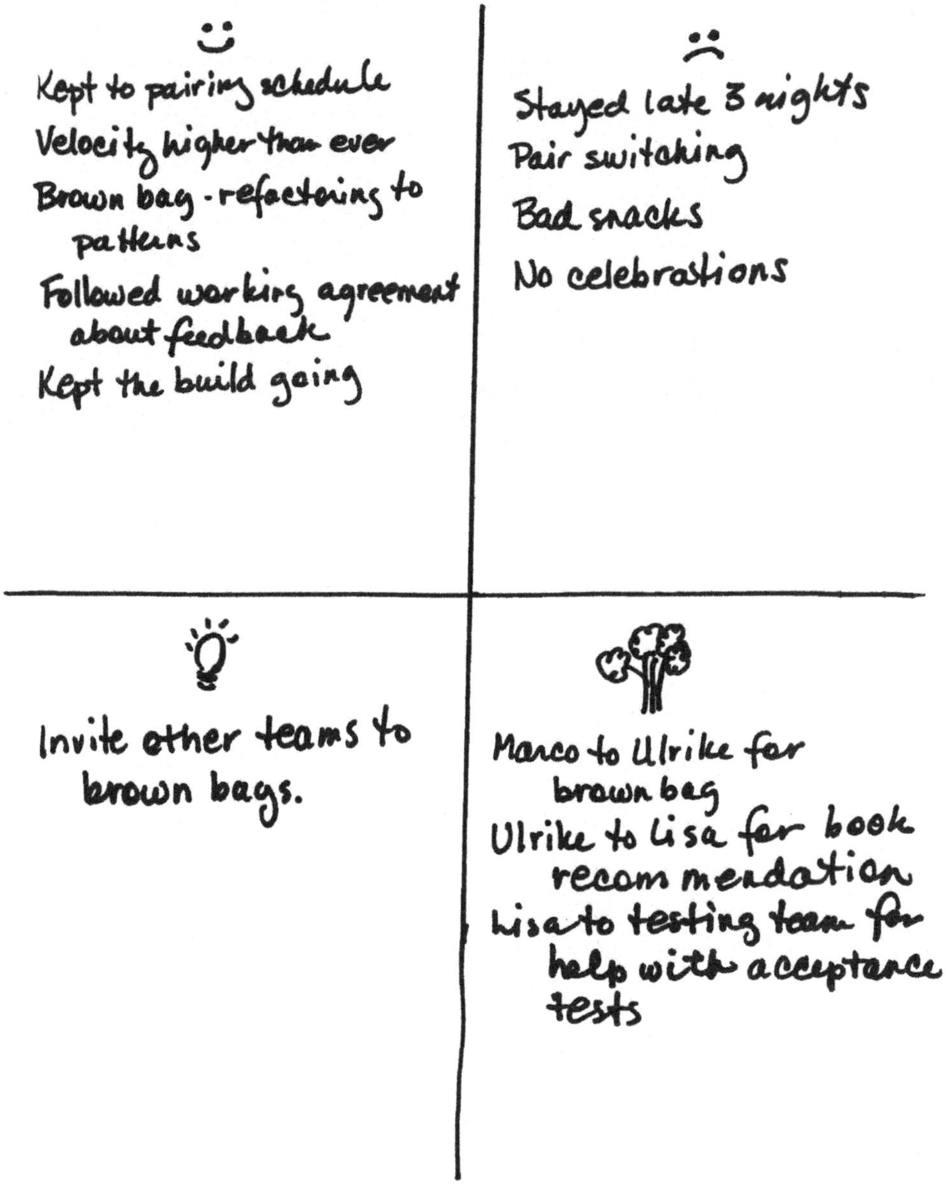

:)

Kept to pairing schedule
Velocity higher than ever
Brown bag - refactoring to
    patterns
Followed working agreement
    about feedback
Kept the build going

:(

Stayed late 3 nights
Pair switching
Bad snacks
No celebrations

Invite other teams to
brown bags.

Marco to Ulrike for
    brown bag
Ulrike to Lisa for book
    recommendation
Lisa to testing team for
    help with acceptance
    tests

Learning Matrix is a quick way to capture insights.

Figure 17—Learning matrix

CHAPTER 7

Activities to Decide What to Do

Deciding What to Do moves the team's focus to the next iteration. In these activities the team members develop proposals for action, identify the highest priority actions, create detailed plans for experiments, and set measurable goals to achieve the results.

You can also use Triple Nickels on page 54 to generate ideas for action.

7.1   Activity: Retrospective Planning Game

Use this to develop action plans in Deciding What to Do in a release, or project retrospective.

Purpose

Develop detailed plans for experiments or proposals.

Time needed

Forty to seventy-five minutes depending on the number of experiments and the size of the group.

Description

Team members work individually or in pairs to brainstorm all the tasks necessary to complete an experiment, improvement, or recommendation. After brainstorming, team members eliminate redundant tasks and fill in gaps. The task are arranged in order, and team members sign up for tasks they will complete.

Steps

1. Introduce the activity by saying, "We're going to work on generating all the tasks needed to have our experiment succeed." Then recap the experiment (improvement, or recommendation).

2. Describe the process:

    Work individually or in pairs to generate all the tasks.

    Form pairs of pairs to compare tasks, eliminate duplicates and fill gaps.

    Cluster the tasks and again check for duplicates and gaps.

    Order the tasks.

3. Form pairs (or not, if there are fewer than eight people do this individually). Hand out sticky notes or index cards and markers.

    Ask the group to write one task per card or sticky, leaving the bottom half blank. Show an example (see one below).

4. Form pairs of pairs (or pairs if the previous step was done individually). Reiterate the instruction: Compare tasks, eliminate duplicates and write any new tasks you realize are missing. It's okay to re-write or consolidate as needed.

If the group is larger than 16, have the groups of four form groups of eight and do another round of comparing, adding, and eliminating duplicates before proceeding to the next step.

5. Invite the group to post and cluster the tasks on a whiteboard or wall. If they've used cards, they can cluster them using a table. Once again, compare, look for duplicates, and add any new tasks that the team realizes are missing.

    Leave room on the left side of the wall or whiteboard. The team will use this in the next step when they order the tasks.

6. Order the cards. Start by asking: "Which task must be done first?" Move that task to the extreme left of the working surface. Then ask, "Are there any tasks that can be done simultaneously with this task?" Place those above or below the first task.

    Ask which task needs to be done next. Place that to the right of the first task.

7. Invite team members to sign up for tasks by writing their names on the bottom half of the task cards. Or if it's more appropriate, bring the tasks into the next iteration planning meeting.

Materials and preparation

Sticky notes or index cards. Markers. A wall, whiteboard, or other flat working surface.

If your team hasn't done this kind of planning before, prepare an example of a task card.

Example

The Retrospective Planning Game activity helps teams take vaguely stated goals for improvement and turn them into concrete tasks and action steps.

In the retrospective for their second release, a team developing software for scanners decided to work on new ideas for reviewing their 1400 automated tests. Their current approach was too slow and stalling team progress. They brainstormed and determined a few possible approaches. The retrospective leader invited team members to choose which approach interested them the most. Groups of two or three interested volunteers worked to identify action steps and wrote one action each on several large sticky notes.

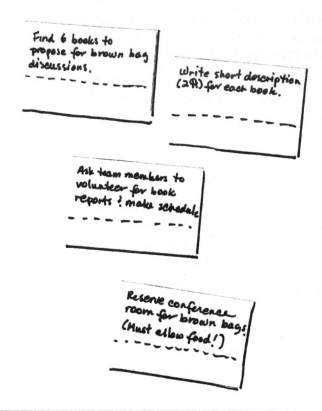

Figure 18—Task cards for the Retrospective Planning Game

They put the sticky notes on the wall for sorting. The retrospective leader asked them to look for duplications or missing steps or tasks. When the whole team agreed the right set of actions were on the wall, they began to look for dependencies between tasks. They used lengths cut from a ball of yarn and bits of tape to make a visual link between dependent tasks.

They discussed which actions were the best fit with their next iteration plan, which would make the most difference and what risks they could anticipate.

The team left the retrospective with a clear idea about what tasks to include in planning the next release. They had created manageable actions out of a huge improvement goal and knew what they had to do to reduce the risks.

7.2   Activity: SMART Goals

Use this activity to Decide What to Do in an iteration, release, or project retrospective.

Purpose

Translate ideas into priorities and action plans. Develop specific measurable actions.

Time needed

Twenty to sixty minutes depending on the size of the group.

Description

Focus the team's attention on developing goals that are Specific, Measurable, Attainable, Relevant, and Timely. Goals that have these characteristics are more likely to reach fruition.

Steps

1. Introduce the activity by leading a short discussion on the importance SMART goals. Point out that goals that aren't specific, measurable, relevant, and timely tend to fizzle.

2. Point to the SMART characteristics written on a white board or flip chart. Offer an example of a SMART goal: "Our goal is to pair program at least 5 hours a day starting next Monday. We'll rotate pairs daily. We'll create a chart with the pairing schedule, and review it at our next retrospective." Contrast a non-SMART goal: "We should pair more." Note: choose an example that isn't related to the experiments or improvements the team is working on.

3. Form groups around the items that the team prioritized to work on. Ask each group to develop a SMART goal for the initiative, and identify 1–5 action steps to accomplish the goal. Monitor activity.

4. Ask each group to report their goal and plan. After each report, confirm with the rest of the group that the goals are, in fact, SMART. Invite the group to offer refinements.

Materials and preparation

Flip chart paper or a white board. Markers. A flip chart listing the characteristics of SMART goals (see below).

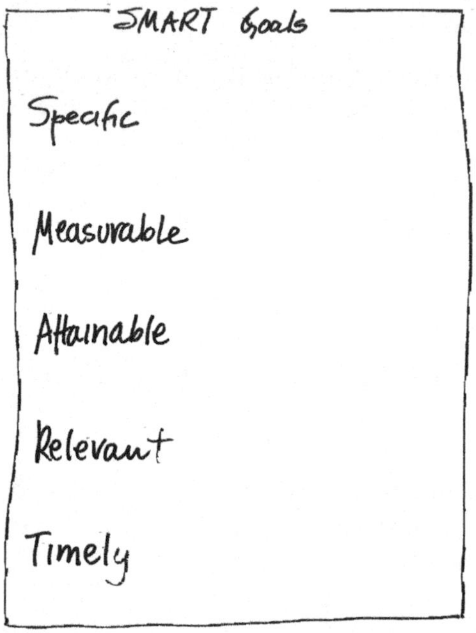

SMART Goals

Specific

Measurable

Attainable

Relevant

Timely

Goals that don't meet these criteria don't get done.

Figure 19—List the characteristic of SMART goals

Example

Time and time again, we see the difference between groups who have only a vague idea of what they want to accomplish and those who have detailed goals. The groups that formulate goals to meet these criteria accomplish their goal (at least most of the time). The other groups don't. Sometimes the other groups don't even start because the goal is too vague to generate forward momentum.

7.3 Activity: Circle of Questions

Use this activity to Decide What to Do in an iteration, release or end of project retrospective.

Purpose

Help team choose an experiment or action steps for the next iteration, particularly when team members need to listen to one another.

Time needed

Thirty+ minutes, depending on team size.

Description

Team members engage in a question asking and answering process to reach consensus on next steps.

Steps

1. Invite team members to sit in a circle. Introduce the activity. "Sometimes the best way to find answers is to ask questions. We'll ask questions to find what we want to do as a result of what we've learned in this retrospective. We'll go around the circle until we are satisfied with our answers or until at least [timebox] minutes have passed."

2. Turn to the person on your left and ask a question. You might start with "From your perspective, what is the highest priority for us to try in the next iteration?" The team member answers, from his or her perspective, to the best of his or her knowledge and ability. Then that team member becomes the questioner, turning to the person on his or her left to ask a question that extends the previous discussion or starts a new one.

   The new respondent answers and, then in turn, asks a question and so on around the circle until the group is satisfied that their questions about the topic have been heard and considered, and a consensus for action has emerged.

Materials and preparation

Set chairs in a circle with no table in the middle. Have a flip chart nearby for recording outcomes.

Examples

When leading Circle of Questions in a team, we stop the activity only at a point when the whole circle has been completed at least twice. Whether you go around two, three, four (or more) times, continue until each person has had the chance to ask and answer a question. Stopping short of completing the circle sends a message that some folks' views are more important than others.

Powerful insights and direction for action emerge from this activity. Encourage everyone to pause for a few seconds before asking or answering a question. The experience of focused attentive listening, and being listened to by the team, provokes team members' best ideas.

Trust is an important factor on self-organizing, Agile teams. The Circle of Questions activity can be one of the few times that a team devotes equal attention to each of its members. Honoring each other's words this way helps to build trust in team working relationships.

7.4   Activity: Short Subjects

Use to Decide What to Do in an iteration retrospective.

Purpose

Help to discover differing perspectives on how the team is doing and provide variety in very short retrospectives.

Time Needed

Twenty to thirty minutes.

Description

The team brainstorms lists of ideas for action, in response to prompts on the 2–3 flip charts. Titles may include:

- What Worked Well/Do Differently Next Time, a.k.a. as WWWDD
- Keep/Drop/Add
- Stop Doing/Start Doing/Keep Doing (a.k.a. StoStaKee)
- Start/Stop/Stay
- Smiley/Frowny
- Mads/Sads/Glads
- Prouds/Sorries
- Plus/Delta (on the iteration)

Steps

1. Post the flip charts. Give team members 3-5 minutes to reflect privately on the iteration and write notes.

2. Lead a brainstorming and record ideas. Keep going until all the comments team members think are important have been posted on the charts. Remember to wait through one or two silences for the next burst of comments.

3. Ask the team to identify the top 20% of the items-those items they believe have the potential for the greatest benefit. Lead a short open discussion, then vote with dots. (See Priority Dots.)

4. If there are more than 2–3 high priority items, reduce the remaining number of issues for action to a manageable few.

5. Keep the brainstormed lists for historical review at subsequent iteration retrospectives to help identify areas of persistent issues.

Materials and Preparation

Prepare a flip charts with titles for discussion, changing the titles from iteration to iteration. As the team becomes over-familiar with one format, move on to another.

Variations

Use any of these in Closing to reflect on the retrospective processes and outcomes.

Give sticky notes to team members to fill out and stick on the corresponding chart instead of brainstorming lists. Sort notes into clusters of like ideas and name the clusters.

Examples

Teams have an unfortunate tendency to choose one of these schemes and use that activity as the only activity in their retrospectives, or b) choose one and use it time after time. It's a fine activity in its place, but doesn't provide rich ideas when used as a stand alone retrospective.

We've heard iteration retrospectives referred to as "heartbeat" retrospectives—part of the regular rhythm and lifeblood of the project team. Listening to a heartbeat or taking a pulse gives indicators about the health of a person, and iteration retrospectives diagnose the health of the team. That said, listening to heartbeats, even our own, can become monotonous.

When you're holding retrospectives iteration after iteration, particularly when the iterations are short, one or two week increments, teams get bored when the same activities or approaches to discussion show up week after week.

Use the variety provided by Short Subjects to change the perspective on discussions. Add your own flavor. Make up categories that fit for the team. (Continue, Integrate, Refactor?)

Activities to Close the Retrospective

Closing the retrospective provides moments for continuous improvement, for reflecting on what happened during the retrospective, and for expressing appreciation. Activities from other chapters (Satisfaction Histogram, Team Radar, Learning Matrix, and Short Subjects), the four-step debriefing method, and other suggestions from the appendix on debriefing can be adapted for use in closing, as well as the activities listed in this chapter.

8.1 Activity: +/Delta

Use this to close an iteration, release, or project retrospective.

Purpose

To retrospect on the retrospective and identify strengths and improvements.

Time Needed

Ten to twenty minutes, depending on the size of the group.

Description

The team identifies strengths (do more of) and changes for the next retrospective.

Steps

1. Introduce the activity by saying, "Before we finish, let's identify what we want to keep and what we want to change for our next retrospective."

2. Draw a *T* on a piece of flip chart paper (cf. Figure 20, *+/Delta is a simple way to improve your retrospectives*, on page 111). Announce the timebox (five to fifteen minutes).

3. Ask the group to shout out strengths and changes. Capture them verbatim. Stop when the ideas stop flowing, or at the end of the timebox. Wait a few seconds. Often the best ideas come after the silence.

4. Thank the group for their candid feedback. Compare the list to those from (recent) previous retrospectives to see whether there are patterns.

Materials and Preparation

Flip chart paper or a white board. Markers.

Example

As retrospective leaders we seek to improve our own methods and skills at leading retrospectives. So we ask for feedback from the group. Two thoughts:

- *Delta* is the Greek alphabet symbol for change. +/Delta (what worked well that we should keep for future retrospectives, what should change in future retrospectives) seeks feedback and ideas to focus on the future, rather than asking the group to pass judgment on the retrospective that is concluding. Even when we want to increase our skills at leading retrospectives, a load of judgments about what was good or bad about what

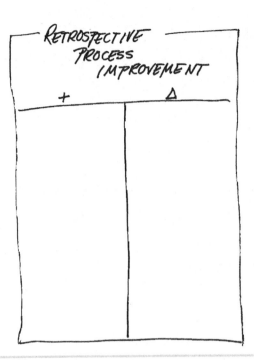

Figure 20—+/Delta is a simple way to improve your retrospectives

just happened can feel demoralizing. When a retrospective leader has devoted effort to plan and facilitate the group, she may be tired at the end. +/Delta helps to ensure the feedback the leader gets is useful yet nonblaming.

- We've had teams "generously" give us more feedback and suggestions for change than we could use. Just as our teams need to focus on only one or two experiments for the next iteration, we need a way to keep from being overwhelmed with too many suggestions for improving our retrospectives.

The one flip chart, the T-structure of +/Delta, helps to limit the amount of feedback from any one retrospective. When you get to the bottom of the page on either side of the *T*, you're done. Thank the team sincerely for their feedback and help, and close the retrospective. If there's more to say, a team member will seek you out later, or the thought will come up again next time.

8.2 Activity: Appreciations

Use this to close an iteration, release, or project retrospective.

Purpose

To allow team members to notice and appreciate each other. End the retrospective on a positive note.

Time Needed

Five to thirty minutes, depending on the size of the group.

Description

Team members appreciate other team members for helping them, contributing, to the team, solving a problem, etc. Offering an appreciation is optional (*The Satir Model: Family Therapy and Beyond* [Sat91]).

Steps

1. Introduce the activity by saying, "As we end, let's take this opportunity to notice and appreciate how others have contributed during this session and during the iteration/release/project."

2. Demonstrate the form with a team member. Even though it's a demonstration, choose a person that you can speak to sincerely.

   Say the name and then say, "I appreciate you for_____." Fill in the blank with something about the person or something he or she did. You can briefly describe the impact on you.

   Here's an example: "Jody, I appreciate you for helping me learn the X feature. You really helped me get up to speed."

3. Sit down. Wait. Someone will offer an appreciation. When the appreciations slow down, wait. Allow silence. Some people need time to work up to this.

   Close when a minute or so has passed with no one speaking up.

Materials and Preparation

None. You may want to write the form on a flip chart or white board.

Example

One time when we explained this activity in a retrospective workshop, a manager said, "Our developers will never go for that! They're engineers. Anyway, they know we appreciate them." The manager never noticed the engineers shaking their heads in disagreement.

It is true that many people shy away from this activity. That's too bad; every time we use this activity, people make genuine and heartfelt appreciations. And you can see people light up when they receive an appreciation.

One group we worked with told us later that they'd done only one thing as a result of their retrospective. "What did you do?" we asked. "We started using appreciations at our weekly meeting, and that's changed the way we relate to each other. We don't have fights anymore. We still disagree, but now we know that we really do value each other. And that makes the tough times easier."

Enough said.

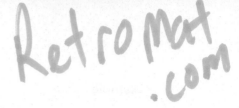

8.3   Activity: Temperature Reading

Use this while setting the stage or closing an iteration retrospective.

Purpose

Check on "where we're at." A practical way to process what is happening for the group (*A Resource Handbook for Satir Concepts* [Sch90]).

Time needed

Ten to thirty minutes, depending on the size of the group.

Description

Team members report on what's happening for them and what they want.

Steps

1. Introduce the activity by saying "Let's look at what's happening in our group. You can contribute in any of the sections, but participation is voluntary. The aim is to hear from others, so no commenting on another's contribution."

2. Point to the poster (see Figure 21, *The Elements of Temperature Reading*, on page 115) with the parts of the Temperature Reading. Comment on each of the five sections and then allow time for people to comment.

   Appreciations are an opportunity to notice how others have contributed and what they bring to the team. Demonstrate the form by offering a sincere appreciation to someone in the group. The form is "[Name of person], I appreciate you for_____." Add a brief statement of the impact on you.

   New information is a time to share information that may be relevant to the group.

   Puzzles are things we don't understand, but we're curious about. Puzzles don't always have answers.

   Complaints with recommendations allow people to point out what they'd like to be different.

   Hopes and wishes let us say what we hope for (for the retrospective or after the retrospective).

   Wait between each section. Record puzzles and complaints with recommendations on a flip chart or white board.

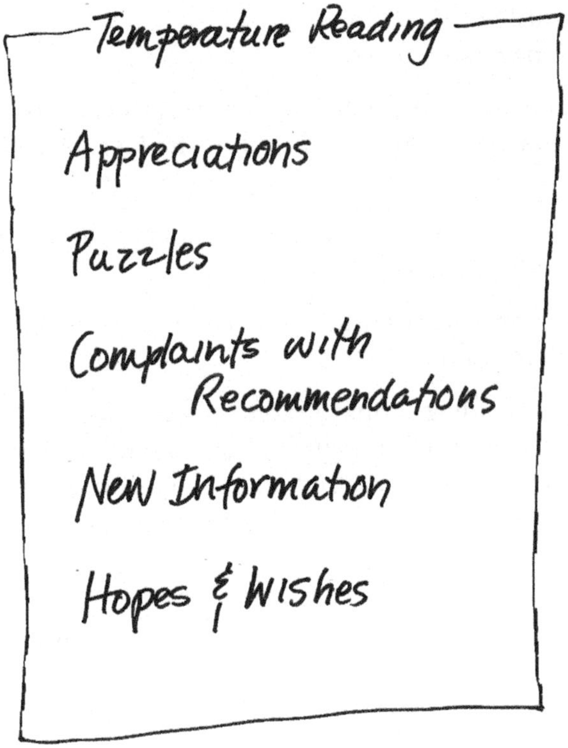

Temperature Reading allows people to include aspects of group life that are usually ignored: appreciations, puzzles, and hopes and wishes.

Figure 21—The Elements of Temperature Reading

Materials and Preparation

Prepare by writing the sections of the Temperature Reading on a flip chart or white board (see Figure 21, *The Elements of Temperature Reading*, on page 115).

Example

There's a trick to leading the Temperature Reading activity. Learn to count silently to yourself. This format is unfamiliar to most people, and it can take them a while to become comfortable with it. Silent counting gives the retrospective leader something to do while waiting, and ensures that people have time to gather their thoughts.

After demonstrating how to give an appreciation, start counting to yourself. Look around the room with an inviting expression as you count. Stay with appreciations until you've counted to 75. Well before then, someone will step forward. If they don't, move on.

One person giving an appreciation usually gets the group going. When the appreciations slow down, count to 20 after the last one. Then move on to puzzles.

Describe puzzles, and start counting to 20. Afterward, use a count of 20 to help wait through each pause.

Once a team has become used to Temperature Readings, they jump right in. You won't get to count.

The Temperature Reading format serves many purposes. We've used it to organize status meetings for a team that met monthly for project planning. The team members stayed energized and focused on the meetings all year. They ended the year with strong working relationships.

8.4 Activity: Helped, Hindered, Hypothesis

Use when closing iteration or release retrospectives.

Purpose

Help the retrospective leader get feedback to improve skills and processes.

Time Needed

Five to ten minutes.

Description

Retrospective leader gathers feedback from team members to discover what helped team members work and learn together during the session, find out what hindered them, and get ideas about what else to try in future retrospectives.

Steps

1. Show the three flip charts, and hand out sticky notes to the team members. "Please help me to become a better retrospective leader. Give me feedback on this retrospective. These three charts represent things about this retrospective that helped you to think as a group and learn about the iteration, things that hindered or got in the way of your thinking or learning, and what hypothesis you might have about things I could do differently to improve our next retrospective."

2. "Use the sticky notes to write your feedback. When you are done please put your initials on each note, and stick them on the appropriate flip chart."

3. End by thanking the team for helping you to improve. Ask whether you may contact team members later if you need clarification or have questions about what they've written.

Materials and Preparation

Prepare three blank flip charts with titles at the top: "Helped," "Hindered," "Hypothesis."

Examples

The Helped, Hindered, Hypothesis (HHH) activity highlights team learning and encourages team members to think about how and what they learn best. As teams focus on whole-team learning, they get better at it.

When a team ended its retrospective with HHH, they noticed that about half the team wanted more individually focused activities and the other half of the team wanted more pair and small group activities. As team members discussed this split and what it could mean for future retrospectives, they realized these differences had implications for their daily work as well. The discussion alerted retrospective leaders to pay attention to what activities they chose for their designs. The team also changed their midweek, hour-long, free-for-all status meetings to fifteen-minute, focused, daily stand-up meetings that better suited the needs of both groups.

8.5   Activity: Return on Time Invested (ROTI)

Use in the closing retrospective phase for iteration or release retrospectives (or at the end of any meeting you'd like to improve).

Purpose

Help generate feedback on the retrospective process and gauge the effectiveness of the session from the team members' perspectives.

Time Needed

Ten minutes.

Description

At the end of retrospective, ask team members to give feedback on whether they spent their time well.

Steps

1. Show the three flip charts to the group, and discuss the types of benefits that might come out of the group process. Types of benefits include decision making (did the retrospective result in decisions that move the team forward?), information sharing (did team members receive useful information or answers to questions?), problem-solving (were team members able to state and solve problems, find alternative solutions, and choose actions?)

2. Going around the circle, ask each team member to say the number that reflects their return on time invested. Record hash marks on the second flip chart.

3. After everyone has responded, ask those who rated the retrospective 2 or higher to say what benefits they received. Then ask those who rated the retrospective 0 or 1, what they wanted but didn't get.

4. Even if many people rated the meeting at 3 or 4, ask the whole group to tell you what to keep or change about the process. Write their answers on a blank flip chart. Express your appreciation for their help in improving the team retrospectives.

Materials and Preparation

Prepare two flip charts. (See Figure 22, *An example of an ROTI chart*, on page 120 and Figure 23, *A sample tally for the ROTI activity*, on page 121.)

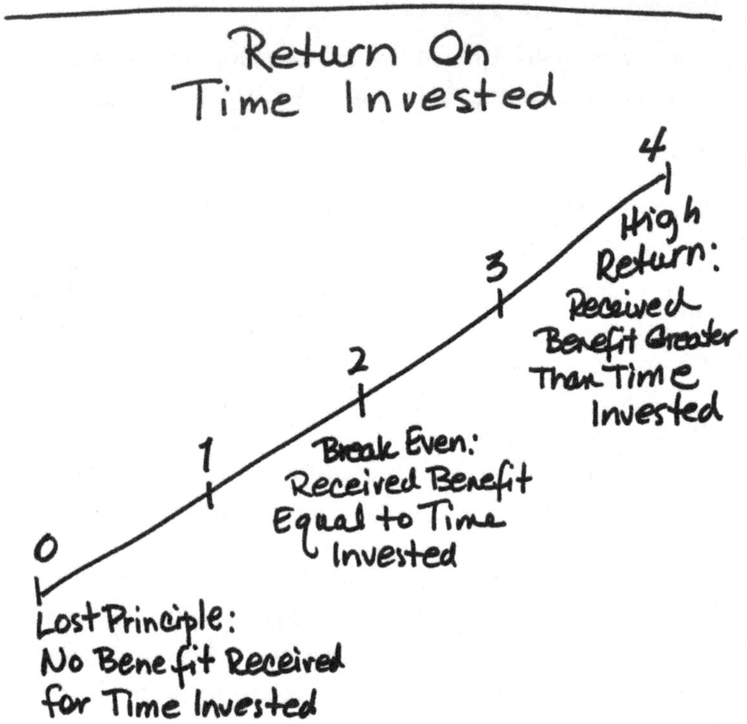

Examining the return on their time invested in retrospectives helps the team make wiser decisions about how they allocate time.

Figure 22—An example of an ROTI chart

Examples

We're happy if most team members feel the meeting was at least a break-even investment. There's always room for improvement, and it's still worthwhile to ask the follow-up questions. One team who gave high ratings to the retrospective found a better meeting room after thinking about what could change.

Don't assume that a rating of 0 means you did a bad job as the retrospective leader. A 0 rating may simply mean the person was distracted by outside circumstances or conditions in the room. Ask questions to discover the thoughts and feelings behind the ratings (*The Roti Method for Gauging Meeting Effectiveness* [Der03a]).

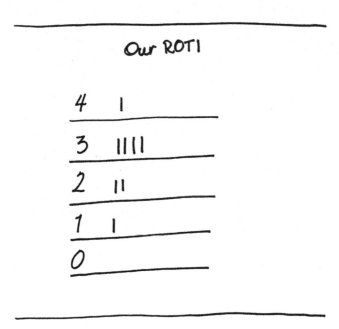

This team finds the retrospectives worthwhile.

Figure 23—A sample tally for the ROTI activity

CHAPTER 9

Releases and Project Retrospectives

Even if your team is performing a retrospective after every iteration, there's reason to have a retrospective after your release and at the end of the project. While iteration retrospectives focus on your team and their issues, release and project retrospectives bring a wider perspective. Release and project retrospectives include people from across the organization—people involved in beta testing, shipping, and supporting the product (among others).

Release and project retrospectives bring together people who must coordinate their work to achieve a goal—deploying software—but may have very different points of view, different missions, and different measures. When groups that cross organizational boundaries come together in a retrospective, there's a chance for organizational learning. It's one thing for a team to identify obstacles—policies, procedures, and practices that inhibit their progress; it's another for the well-intentioned people behind those obstacles to see how they affect the business of building products.

In this chapter, we'll examine how a release or project retrospective is different from an iteration retrospective—from extending the invitation to closing the session. And we'll look at how it's different for the retrospective leader.

9.1 Preparing for Release and Project Retrospectives

Most iteration retrospectives focus solely on the team. At the end of a release or project, include the team and other members of the project community—people who contributed to the effort but weren't part of the core team. You may include managers and additional customers.

Extending the Invitation Beyond Your Team   Your agile team may know and love retrospectives, but the broader project community may not. They may be skeptical, overscheduled, or unaware of what to expect. You have

> ## A Few Definitions
>
> Every time we visit a new organization, we calibrate our decoder rings so we understand how people are using common words that have multiple meanings.
>
> So let's calibrate for retrospectives.
>
> An iteration is a one-week to thirty-day development cycle. The team commits to a goal and creates a small but complete piece of working software. *Complete* means tested, documented, and that the code integrates into the larger product (if there is an existing product).
>
> In Scrum (an Agile method), iterations are called *sprints*.
>
> A release happens when working code—built iteration by iteration—is ready for other people to use. The release may be limited to a group inside the company, such as a specialized testing group or a beta test group. Or the release may make the software available to customers (inside or outside the company).
>
> A project may include one release or several releases. The end of a project usually marks the end of funding and the end of the team.

three tasks: decide who to invite, extend the invitation, and educate new participants.

Releasing a product touches many more people than delivering an increment of working software. Pause to take a broader and deeper look at how you're working with the rest of the organization. Choose participants to fit the goal of the retrospective. Look for people who played a significant role and are willing to share their perspectives.

For one release retrospective, the leader invited Pat and Ron, representatives from Human Resources and Facilities. During the retrospective, Pat and Ron learned how their standard policies had impeded the project. Ron gained an understanding of the urgency behind requests to move machines in the team room. Pat realized that asking for a 26-page performance review for every team member in the middle of a release took the coach out of action for a month. The team heard Ron's point of view and agreed to provide longer lead times for hardware moves. The team learned they needed to enlist the supporting functions early.

As you decide whom to invite, consider how the team interacted with other parts of the organization. Look for areas of friction or support. Invite representatives to learn from both points of view (*Project Retrospectives: A Handbook for Team Reviews* [Ker01]). When it's just not practical to involve everyone in the project community, include as many perspectives as possible by selecting a cross-section.

For a release retrospective consider inviting folks who represent admin support, on-site customers, product owners, the deployment team, the testing group, marketing, technical support, help desk, operations, beta testers, and the project manager.

At the end of project, invite all of the above, the project sponsor, and other management stakeholders (e.g., product development engineering management, program management).

Cross-departmental and other large retrospectives need to strike a balance between inclusion and meaningful results. Helping 50 or 100 people think together requires a different approach than helping 10 or 20 people think together. It's possible to achieve consensus on organizational changes with a very large group; but it requires a different process than a retrospective.

On the other hand, if the project involved 200 people only 20 attend the retrospective, diffusing insights and gaining agreement for improvements is a project in itself.

Given the choice between a large cross-department retrospective with a dubious chance of making real improvement and a retrospective that focuses on the team, go with the team.

An invitation signals that the retrospective is an important event. Don't rely on a standard meeting notice. When you invite people, include the the goal for the particular retrospective, date, time, and any preparation people need to do prior to the session. Provide a contact to answer any questions (Figure 24, *Invitation*, on page 126).

Tip 7: Full-Time Attendance

People push back against full-day meetings. They feel pressured to accomplish daily work and may want to drop by the retrospective when they don't have a another meeting scheduled. Even with the best intentions, drop-ins slow down the process; at worst they derail it. Dropouts send a different, often puzzling, message.

Set the expectation for full-time attendance by explaining that the retrospective follows a structure and each part builds on the next.

Emphasize that the goals of the retrospective are learning, improvement, and action. Make sure people know it's an *invitation* (*Project Retrospectives:*

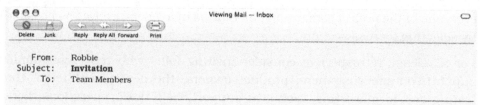

From: Robbie
Subject: **Invitation**
To: Team Members

We've completed our first release, and it's time to discover what we've learned about organizing our development work.

We've scheduled a release retrospective for April 5th, from 8:30–4:00. We will serve lunch. We'll be following a specific structure, and each part will build to the next. Please plan to attend for the entire day.

We'll focus primarily on improving our cross-department communication and coordination. Please think back over the last three months and bring any items that will help us remember what happened during the release.

If you have questions, call Robbie at extension 1234.

Best regards,

Robbie

Figure 24—Invitation

A Handbook for Team Reviews [Ker01]). When people feel pressured to attend, they don't arrive in a collaborative, cooperative mood.

Tip 8:   Coach Managers Prior to the Retrospective

Differences in power and status influence interactions within a retrospective. People who have responsibility for evaluating or appraising the performance of team members—functional managers, project managers, directors, development managers—hold a form of power, and people may defer to them. Meet with each manager before the retrospective to consider his or her roles in discussions. Ask each manager to hold back and create signals to help communicate when a manager is being too assertive.

Up-Front Work   In Chapter 2, *A Retrospective Custom-Fit to Your Team*, on page 15, we describe the preparation you might make for an iteration retrospective, learning about the context and history of the team. For a release or project retrospective, dig deeper. Learn more about how people experienced the project. Your perception counts, of course. And you'll design a better approach with a fuller picture.

Use interviews or a brief questionnaire to learn how people perceive the project. The benefits of up-front preparation are fourfold:

- It starts people reflecting on the project. The questions in an interview or questionnaire start people thinking back about their experience.

- It provides useful background. You will learn more about the context and understand more about the project. You'll learn something about the people involved and how they view the release or project.

- It sets the tone. The way you phrase questions in an interview or questionnaire tells people something about how the retrospective will be. If your questions are open and curious, you'll convey that mind-set for the retrospective. On the other hand, if your questions are closed and seeking fault, you'll condition people to expect blame and narrow thinking in the retrospective.

- It helps you tailor the design. If you know there are certain problems or conflicts, you can select activities that will help the group talk about them effectively. For example, when one retrospective leader interviewed the extended team for a release retrospective, the recurring theme was distrust between developers and management. The retrospective leader included an activity to help the developers express their concerns to their managers.

If the group is small, interview the individuals in person or on the phone. For a larger group, develop a short questionnaire and email it. Specify an early return date if you really want it back.

Choose five or six questions from the following list. Arrange them to flow and make logical sense for your interview or questionnaire. Test the questions by answering them yourself before you try them with the project community. You may not know the content of the answer; the point is to make sure the questions are not so ambiguous that no one will be able to answer them.

- What are the three to five topics that you think you must raise at this retrospective?

- What is the best possible outcome you can imagine for this retrospective? For yourself? For future releases? For the organization?

- What would have to happen during or after the retrospective to achieve those outcomes?

- When you look back over this release, what do you consider to be the one or two high points or most energized times? Why did you choose those experiences? What made them memorable?

- What do you value most about your contribution on this release? What do you value most about the contributions of others?

- What puzzles you about the retrospective?

- What else should I ask, and how would you respond?

Tip 9: Who Owns the Issues?

Beware: some participants believe that once they've written the issue down or mentioned it in a conversation, it's no longer their job to bring it up. Make it clear that issues belong to the people who have them, and you are relying on them to raise topics in the retrospective.

If you discover that the group has a tough issue, pay extra attention to supporting the team. Your job is to create an environment so that the group can bring up tough topics. Put special emphasis on setting the stage, and be prepared to handle emotional situations. (See "Managing Group Dynamics" in Chapter 3, "Leading Retrospectives".)

Explain that you'll use the information that you gather to design the approach. Assure people that the information is confidential, and keep it that way. If you do plan to summarize and share the information with the group during the retrospective, say so. Take care to protect individual identities.

9.2 Including Cross-Organizational Perspectives

Iteration retrospectives emphasize the team, its methods, and its interactions. Release and project retrospectives include the broader organizational perspective. While organizational issues may come up in an iteration retrospective, in a release or project retrospective cross-organizational issues are the main focus.

Setting the Stage   Setting the stage works the same for most retrospectives. Cover the same bases as for an iteration retrospective. Even if your team has working agreements, work with the entire group to establish the agreements that this group will abide by for this retrospective. Pay special attention to reminding people that the goal of the retrospective is learning, and fixing problems, not blaming.

Gathering Data   Make sure the data-gathering activities explicitly include perspectives outside the team. One way to do this is to name categories of data such as technology and tools, people and teams, process, and organizational systems. Another is to create an event time-line that specifies each organization present in the retrospective. See variations on Timeline in Chapter 5, *Activities to Gather Data*, on page 49.

Generating Insights   Because people are in different parts of the organization, they see things differently. Their interests—what's important to them—are different. Being aware of these differences helps people work more effectively in the organization. Listen for surprises and contradictory interpretations. Pay attention to forming small groups that focus cross-functional perspectives.

Deciding What to Do   In an iteration retrospective, the team takes action on issues that are within their control. But releases usually involve people from other teams and departments. The problems identified often cross organizational boundaries—they're system problems.

The people in the room may not be able to fix system problems, but they can influence and make proposals. People have control when they can directly change the situation on their own. For example, the team's daily technical decisions and working agreements are within their control. Teams have influence where they have access to someone who has control and can educate and persuade that person or group. For example, a team may not control facilities and furniture, but they can educate the Facilities department about their need for team rooms. They can help managers see the true cost of policies. Analyzing spheres of influence and control help make proposals realistic.

Effective proposals don't just tell other people what they "ought" to do. They describe the issue, pose potential solutions, offer participation in solutions, and invite joint problem solving. If you want another group to help your team or change their ways, help them see what's in it for them, not only what's in it for your team.

It's still important to create action plans for individual development and team improvements. People need to walk out of the retrospective with concrete actions they can accomplish.

Choose an action—even a small one—that people in the room can complete before the retrospective is over. Action begets action.

Guidelines for Action Plans

Every action step needs a verb. Without a verb, it's not an action.

Every action needs someone to own it—one person who commits to carrying the action forward.

Small steps lead to quicker action. Aim for action steps that one person can finish in a week or less.

Due dates drive action. An end date leads to completion. Open-ended tasks tend to stay that way—open and not ended.

Check that actions are Specific, Measurable, Achievable, Relevant, and Timely —SMART.

Define what "done" means for each action and how it will be communicated to the team.

An action plan needs to meet all these criteria.

Tip 10: The Team Owns the Report

The person paying for a large retrospective may want a written report. The report should come from the team, not the retrospective leader. As part of the closing, decide who will create the report. When a retrospective leader writes the report, it reduces team ownership.

Closing the Retrospective   For an iteration retrospective, the team can follow up on themselves. In a larger retrospective, assign follow-up responsibility for proposals and cross-organizational plans. Most often, managers, team leads, or coaches sign up for these tasks.

Choose a closing activity that helps people reflect on their experience, solidify personal insights, and acknowledge each other's contributions.

9.3 Leading Release and Project Retrospectives

Coaches and team leads may lead iteration retrospectives. But when it comes to the release or project retrospective, all team members have part of the story and need to participate, not lead. Enlist a lead or coach from another team or bring in a facilitator from outside the team. Likewise, if you've led iteration retrospectives, other teams may call on you to lead their release retrospectives.

If leading a large retrospective is a one-time event for you, find a mentor. Collaborate on the design, and seek advice on managing a larger group for a longer time. If you plan to do more than one large retrospective, invest in training for yourself.

Here are some differences to consider:

Managing Activities   Many activities that work for iteration retrospectives will work in release or project retrospectives. The trick is to use small groups so that people can actually converse rather than attempting discussions with the entire group.

Managing Dynamics   People are people. You'll see the same behaviors in a large group as in a small group. But the effects are more pronounced. When things go awry, they go bad faster and with more explosive power. The retrospective leader must attend to the process and dynamics. Stay on top of working agreements, and be prepared to name disruptive behavior.

Watch for side conversations in large groups. Side conversations may indicate hidden information, factions, or that someone is undermining the session. Refer to working agreements that touch on full participation or interruptions. Suggest creating a new working agreement to address side conversations, or ask the group how best to handle the behavior.

Of course, most side conversations are not sinister. But side conversations distract and signal disrespect for the current speaker and the process.

Here's how one retrospective leader handled a side conversation that disrupted the retrospective: When Charley and Ron snickered as Fran gave her subgroup report, Sidney paused the report and asked Charley and Ron, "I notice you're having a conversation. Is this information the rest of the group needs to know?" Charley admitted sheepishly that he'd been telling Ron a joke. Sidney admitted he'd been distracted and asked whether that was true for others in the group. When several people nodded, he asked for a working agreement about side conversations. Intervening like this usually solves the problem.

Or, you could say, "One conversation, please."

In either case, don't bring up grade-school memories by demanding to hear the joke, see the note, or share what they've been saying with the group.

Managing Time   In a longer retrospective, everything takes longer. Debriefing, moving between activities, taking breaks, and small group reports all take more time. The structure remains the same, but you'll deal with more people and more complex issues. Especially when there has been conflict, controversy, or an utter failure, allow more time, and consider bringing in an experienced facilitator.

Plan on formal breaks every ninety minutes to two hours. People will still get up to break if they really need to, but this reduces the constant leaving-and-returning movement in the group. Take breaks at natural pause points rather than setting a schedule by the clock. Announce at the beginning that you'll break every ninety minutes or so, and then ask the group to tell you when they need a respite.

Here's an example of a project retrospective.

The team just finished their twenty-fourth one-week iteration. The team delivered the product ahead of schedule and they received a bonus! The team has been doing regular iteration retrospectives and now wants to look back over the project to study what worked and spread the word. Since the team tried several new methods during the project, they want to maintain momentum, even though some of the team will be reassigned to new projects.

The team wants to invite the extended team to learn more about engaging the rest of the organization. The retrospective leader goes through the following thought process while jotting down notes (see Figure 25, *Retrospective leader's notes for a full-day retrospective*, on page 133) and creating an agenda (see Figure 26, *Agenda for a full-day retrospective*, on page 135).

Decision: What is the goal?

We want to learn from perspectives outside the core team and build on success. We also want to maintain momentum.

Decision: Who will attend?

Team, customer, external testing group, operations support, and tech writers. The total number of people in the retrospective will be twenty.

Why? We want to obtain feedback from outside the team and let other people see how we worked and solved problems.

Decision: How long?

A full day.

Why? We'll need time to explore multiple perspectives.

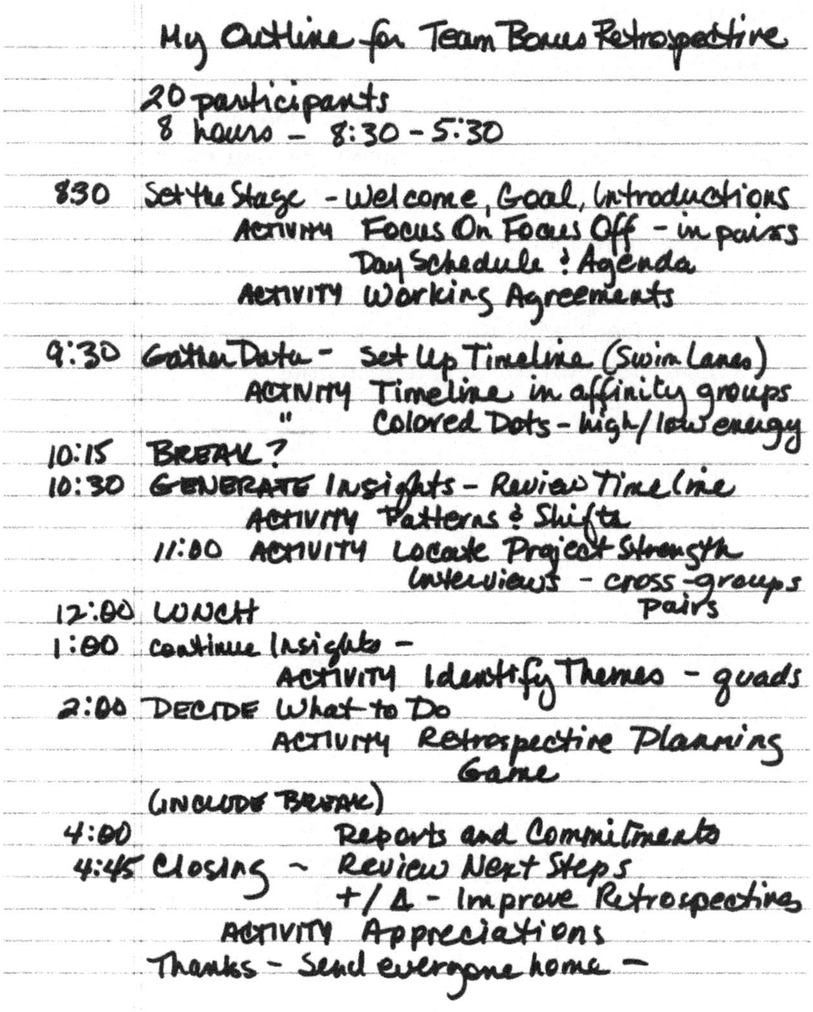

My Outline for Team Bonus Retrospective

20 participants
8 hours – 8:30 – 5:30

830 Set the Stage - Welcome, Goal, Introductions
        ACTIVITY Focus On Focus Off - in pairs
                  Day Schedule & Agenda
        ACTIVITY Working Agreements

9:30 Gather Data - Set Up Timeline (Swim Lanes)
        ACTIVITY Timeline in affinity groups
           "   Colored Dots - high/low energy
10:15 BREAK?
10:30 GENERATE Insights - Review Timeline
        ACTIVITY Patterns & Shifts
  11:00 ACTIVITY Locate Project Strength
                   Interviews - cross-groups
12:00 LUNCH   pairs
1:00 continue Insights -
        ACTIVITY Identify Themes - quads
2:00 DECIDE What to Do
        ACTIVITY Retrospective Planning
                  Game
     (INCLUDE BREAK)
4:00   Reports and Commitments
4:45 Closing ~ Review Next Steps
                 +/Δ - Improve Retrospectives
        ACTIVITY Appreciations
     Thanks - Send everyone home —

Figure 25—Retrospective leader's notes for a full-day retrospective

Decision: Where will we hold the retrospective?

Large training room in the corporate training facility. The occupancy rating is fifty. All furniture is movable. We'll need a large enough space to accommodate twenty people and allow people to move and work in small groups.

Decision: How will we set up the room?

Chairs in a circle. A circle will allow everyone to see each other to start the session. Later move into small group work.

Phase: Set the Stage

Activity: Focus On/Focus Off

Why? Help the group establish a mind-set of looking at the issues without assigning blame. Fosters open discussion. Reassures people who haven't been to retrospectives before.

Activity: Working Agreements

Why? After the opening (review goal, schedule) establish working agreements, because people haven't done this kind of work together before and not all the groups have their own working agreements.

Phase: Gather the Data

Activity: Timeline with Swim Lanes

Why? To re-create the chronology and events of the release and show how the release looked to different departments

Activity: Color Code Dots

Why? Reveal how people experienced the different events in the timeline.

Phase: Generate Insights

Activity: Patterns and Shifts

Why? We want to understand when energy/morale shifted and identify points that stand out (high energy, low energy, or mixed). This should help us see what changes had the most effect and where we overcame obstacles.

Activity: Locate Strengths

Why? We want to build on what worked in high points and focus on how different areas worked together.

Activity: Identify Themes

Why? After the interviews, we'll look for common threads and discern the best ideas.

Phase: Decide What to Do

Activity: Retrospective Planning Game

Why? Hear everyone's ideas about what stories they should tell and converge on most significant practices/interactions to carry forward.

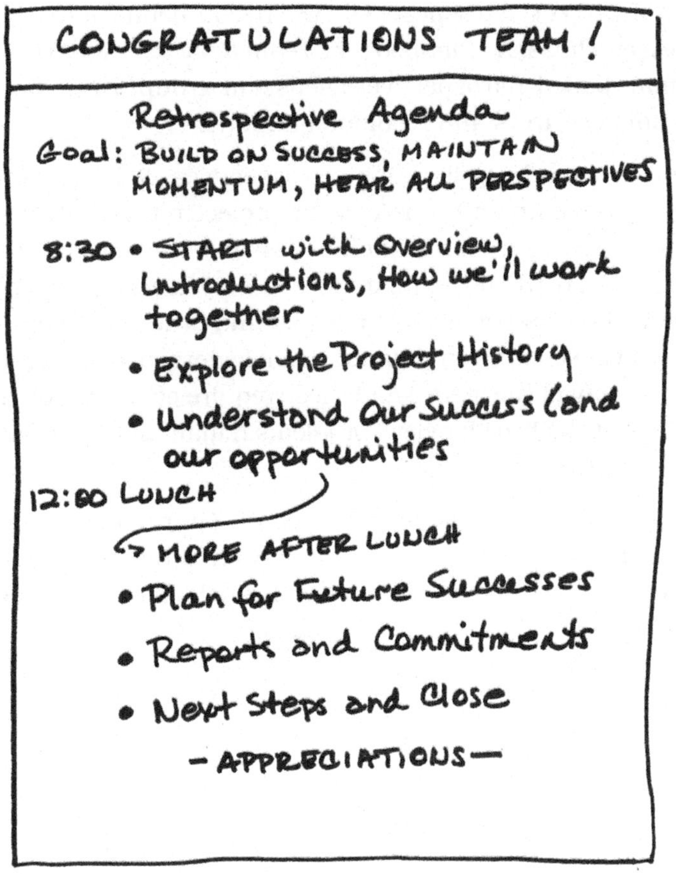

Figure 26—Agenda for a full-day retrospective

Phase: Close the Retrospective

Activity: +/Delta

Why? improve the retrospective. We know what works for iteration retrospective, and this will help us see how to better involve groups outside our team.

Activity: Appreciations

Why? Acknowledge contributions inside and outside the core team.

9.4 A Retrospective at Every Ending

Since this book is focused on short retrospectives that follow every iteration, we haven't covered the release and project retrospectives in depth. We've simply pointed out some of the major differences. If you want to learn more about end-of-project retrospectives, we recommend Norm Kerth's book *Project Retrospectives: A Handbook for Team Reviews* [Ker01]. You can also join the email-based retrospective discussion group. And you can always contact us for resources and recommendations.

Even if you've been doing iteration retrospectives, it's still worth the time and energy to have an end-of-release or project retrospective. People look at different issues and learn different lessons when they take a longer, broader view. Even when the team doesn't stay together, people take that learning with them to benefit other teams and other projects. Release and project retrospectives uncover organizational factors, policies, and procedures that get in the way of the team—and these require coordination across areas to solve. Without the broader view, problems remain hidden or are attributed to the wrong source.

So, hold a retrospective at every ending point. Your teams and your organization will learn and improve as they step back and reflect. Help your team manage their actions, and support them through change. We'll tell you how in the next chapter.

CHAPTER 10

Make It So

Productive teams judge retrospectives by their results.

It would be lovely if we could just say "Make it so" for every change, like Captain Jean-Luc Picard on the Starship Enterprise. But "Make it so" isn't enough. Action plans set the stage for results. Incorporating experiments into iteration work plans makes sure they receive attention. And sometimes it's still not enough.

If you've ever tried to change a personal habit (nail biting, for example) you know that it's virtually impossible unless you have something else to replace the old behavior. It's easier to add a new behavior than extinguish an old one. The same is true for teams and organizations.

At their retrospective, Lynn's team resolved to stop jumping into coding without a plan. But at the next iteration planning meeting, two team members popped open their laptops to share the code they'd worked on over the weekend. They believed they were giving the team a head start.

Lynn reminded everyone about their agreement and shared several ideas for planning that he'd read on an Agile discussion group. The team agreed to stick to their resolution and try Lynn's ideas for planning. As the team began talking through the work they needed to do, the team realized that the code written over the weekend didn't contribute to the team's goal for the iteration— it was wasted effort.

Without a replacement (planning ideas, in this case), the team had no alternative but to fall back on their old behaviors.

Any new behavior feels awkward at first. People develop ease through practice—whether learning a new tennis serve or learning coding in a new language. Provide support and reassurance that it's okay to make mistakes as people try new skills.

10.1 Provide Support

The work of creating a change isn't done when the retrospective is over. Even small changes need to be nurtured and supported. Support comes in different forms: reinforcement, empathy, learning opportunities, practice opportunities, and reminders. Certain kinds of support can come from the team—empathy and reminders, for example. But other support requires resources and a budget. Team leads, coaches, and managers have responsibility for obtaining support that involves expenditure.

Reinforcement   Change is difficult. Support your team (and yourself) by noticing progress. Give encouragement on what is going well: "Our new unit tests are helping us keep the build clean—way to go!" When you encourage your team, you acknowledge the challenges and boost morale.

Provide information on what's going well to help your team recognize that they are making progress. Be sure the feedback describes behavior and states the impact: "I noticed that yesterday we stayed on track in our stand-up meeting. We agreed to stick to our four questions, and we did. That really helped me see what the obstacles were."

Empathy   Acknowledge that people's feelings of loss or frustration are valid. Here's how Fred, a team lead, mishandled the situation when a team member came to talk to him about a change. Fred listened as Katie explained how she felt about giving up her private cubicle when the team decided to move into an open work space. "I've thought about it," Fred responded, "and there's no reason for you to feel that way." This is *not* empathy. Acknowledge the other's point of view and feelings (without agreeing to fix the situation). Simply saying "I hear you" can be enough.

Learning Opportunities   Demonstrate support for exploration and learning. Your team may need to learn new skills to succeed with the experiments they've chosen in their action plans. Organize brown-bag lunches and sharing sessions where team members can learn from each other. Provide lists of web resources and articles for team members to investigate new ideas. Look for informal mentors inside and outside the team. Encourage pair programming to learn new coding languages and techniques. You can do all this without a budget.

Be willing to spend money to support the change. Not every skill can be learned from website or an article. Invest in training to build a foundation for new skills. Build a library so your team has ready access to resources.

Practice Opportunities People need practice to gain proficiency. One way is to turn the team loose on the product to try something new. Another option is to make a formal practice space using a short-short project, a practice area, or a Hello World program.

Create a short-short project—one lasting a day or two, or even less—to explore possible solutions or try a new method. If your team is having trouble timeboxing, starting with something small like a short-short project can serve double duty. The time limit on the short-short project creates an explicit checkpoint where the team can assess their learning and decisions about the experiment.

A practice area is a place where the team can try something new without affecting the real product. The practice area can be a special test or development area that's not used for current product development.

Encourage the team to try Hello World programs. Hello World programs are simple—typically they do nothing more than print or display "Hello World." But they can test development environments and configurations and find problems quickly (or confirm that the basic concept works).

Reminders Big visible charts and check-ins are reminders that help your team focus on changes. For example, Terry's team decided to they needed to refactor more often. They created a large chart where each team member posted a green dot when they finished a refactoring task. At the end of each day, they reviewed the chart and discussed the results. The chart kept refactoring conspicuous.

A check-in lets the team report on what they're doing with a particular change. Keep the questions and answers short: "In a word or two, how are we doing on estimation?" Use the responses as a gauge of how the new practice is going.

10.2 Share Responsibility for Making Changes

When one person consistently grabs responsibility for action items, three problems emerge:

- Your team may come to look upon one team member as a heroic rescuer. The rescuer may rely on the heroic role for emotional reasons—to the detriment of the team. Whether the team relies on a rescuer or a rescuer seeks the role, the dynamic kills collaboration and shared ownership.

- When a formal or informal leader consistently takes responsibility (except for system problems outside the team), that person teaches the team to be helpless victims. Collaborating to make improvements strengthens the team. Taking away that responsibility cripples them.

• When a team consistently assigns responsibility for problem resolution to a subgroup within the team, it creates a perception that the subgroup is the source of all problems. Scapegoating breaks the team. Share responsibility, and rotate change leadership.

10.3 Supporting Larger Changes

Iteration retrospectives usually generate compact changes—changes that the team can accomplish in the next iteration or stepwise over a few iterations. Larger retrospectives can generate broader changes that take longer to implement. Broader changes require more support and more attention to how people respond to change.

People experience predictable transitions as they let go of the old and take on the new, even when they've chosen and planned the change (*The Satir Model: Family Therapy and Beyond* [Sat91], *Managing Transitions: Making the Most of Change* [Bri03]). When a change is perceived as small, people adapt without external support. For larger changes, the transition takes longer and happens at different rates for different people. Understanding the four phases of change will help you support your team.

Four Transitional Phases in a Change

These are the four phases:

Loss   Starting something new always begins with letting go of the old. People experience loss—loss of competence, territory, relationships, certainty. Excitement about the new may pull them through this phase quickly, or they may take longer to adjust. Either way, they can't, and won't, move forward until they let go.

Chaos   Letting go of the old doesn't mean we fully understand the new. People feel confused and strive to reorient themselves during a time of change. They explore how things will change and what this new way will mean for them. Along with confusion, chaos may spark innovation and creativity. People may invent new approaches because the rules aren't settled yet.

Transforming Idea   Eventually, people see or experience how this new way will work for them. Experiments and exploration lead them to a fresh understanding. An outside influence may bring a new perspective. Team members begin to try new behaviors and ideas.

Practice and Integration   An idea is not enough. People need to practice to learn a new skill or adapt to a new structure. Performance may drop initially but will improve with practice.

As people move through the stages of change, help them by attending to these three areas:

What People Value   Identify what team members valued in the old way. Look for ways to carry the value forward while leaving behind what isn't working. By acknowledging what was valuable in the old way, you recognize that people were not stupid or wrong. At some time, someone thought it was a good idea, and it was, then. People move forward more easily when they believe that changing doesn't imply they've been stupid.

For example, during their release retrospective, Lakshmi and her team realized they needed to increase their team size by 50% to keep up demand for their product. They were excited that their products were so successful, but they also felt the loss of their small, cohesive team. As they brought in new people, the team lead worked to clarify the team's values and the practices they wanted to keep. The original team prioritized what was most important to carry forward as they grew into a larger team.

Temporary Structures   Temporary structures help people navigate the chaotic phase between the old way and the new way. Temporary structures can be plans, roles, meetings, methods—any mechanism that bridges the current state and the goal state.

Here's how one team created a temporary structure: Franz and his team worked on high-tech medical devices. During the retrospective after a long, painful project, the team decided to manage risk by moving toward iterative incremental development using XP. They hired a coach and attended immersion training. The business, on the other hand, was skeptical of throwing away their requirements documents and relying on stories written on index cards—with reason. They were heavily regulated.

Rather than give up on XP or resent the business for not trying stories, the team devised a temporary structure. They gratefully accepted the business's requirements document and then turned the requirements into stories, one iteration at a time. At the end of every iteration, they showed the business the software they'd written and explained how the stories related to the requirements. After several iterations, the businesspeople began to see the value of writing requirements as stories and devised a way to trace stories for regulatory purposes.

The temporary structure—translating requirements into stories—enabled the team to move forward toward a desired goal.

Information and Rumor Control   When something changes, people hunger for information about how the change will affect them. When people lack information, they fill in the gaps with their worst fears. Rumors start even on small teams.

Establish a regular mechanism to control rumors during the course of change. Offer new information, assuage fears, uncover rumors, and provide facts.

One team created a Rumor Control Bulletin Board. Whenever a team member heard a rumor, that person wrote it on a card and posted it on the board. Everyone could read the latest rumors and take responsibility for tracking down the facts. Once the facts were known, they were posted too, keeping the rumor mill under control.

In addition, the Rumor Control Bulletin Board telegraphed that much of what people were hearing simply wasn't true. People stopped overreacting to the latest gossip and checked out the facts before passing anything along.

Retrospectives can be a powerful catalyst for change. A major transformation can start from a single retrospective. Incremental improvement is important, too. Celebrate it. It's more than many teams ever achieve.

Facilitation Supplies

Having the right tools makes leading a retrospective easier and more fun. Here are tips about the tools of the trade.

If you facilitate more than a few times a year—and if your team is holding a retrospective after every iteration, you are—assemble a kit that you can pick up and take with you without having to remember and collect everything you'll need.

For iteration retrospectives, bring sticky notes, markers, painters' tape, and dots. Throw these tools in a spare box or tote bag, and you're ready to go.

Here's what's we put in a our kit for longer retrospectives:

- Painters' tape—the kind designed to be on the wall for a week or more without pulling the paint off
- Water-based markers in a variety of dark colors
- Sticky notes—small, medium, and large
- Index cards, 3×5 and larger
- Glue sticks
- Post-it correction tape
- Scissors
- Pocketknife
- Chime, bell, or gong
- Sticky color dots
- Timer
- Calculator

Store it all in a plastic bin, a rolling suitcase, or a cardboard box. Whatever you choose, make it easy to store, find, and transport to the retrospective.

Using cards, sticky notes, markers, and dots helps people see ideas, group ideas, and vote on priorities. Carry scissors or a pocketknife to cut paper to size and open boxes. Bring tape to stick stuff on walls. Glue sticks and correction tape come in handy when you make a mistake on a flip chart. Use a timer to keep track of time. If you're working with a large group, a chime works much better than yelling to get people's attention. Keep a calculator in the box—and hand it to a participant when you need some calculating done.

You'll discover other things that work for you—but this is a good start.

Resources for Supplies   Local office-supply stores stock most of these items. When you want to get fancy, check out these sites:

http://www.artsuppliesonline.com—Buy markers in the colors you use most, without having to get a package with colors that you don't want.

http://www.neuland.biz—Refillable makers and other high-end facilitation supplies with a European flair.

http://www.vis-it.com—Special shapes and sizes of sticky notes.

Tips About Markers   Bring your own markers. Don't rely on what you find in conference rooms or conference centers. Those markers are likely to be white board markers or, worse, dried out and useless.

White board and permanent markers are toxic and can give both you and your team members a headache. Some people are allergic to the chemicals in these markers and actually get sick from them.

Bring markers in dark colors—black, dark blue, dark green, purple, and brown. Lighter colors are fun for highlighting, but yellow is impossible to see from more than a few feet away. Red looks dark but is difficult to read from a distance. Water-based markers are nontoxic and (mostly) washable.

Look for markers with chisel tips, not points. Pointy markers make a line that's too thin to read from across the room.

Capturing a Record   Use a digital camera to take pictures of significant flip charts. If team members are willing, take pictures of them as they work, too. A visual reminder of the retrospective means more than a typed-up report.

While these tools and tips are important, you are your most important tool. No gadget will be more important than your ability to provide a process, manage the flow of ideas, and guide the group to discover their wisdom.

Debriefing Activities

The four-step debriefing method described in Chapter 3, *Leading Retrospectives*, on page 27 works in almost every situation. But just as activities wear out, so do debriefs. After a while, your team will recognize the order of the questions. They may even groan. So here are four other ways to debrief activities.

The One-Question Debrief   Ask, "What's the first thing you want to say about this activity?"

Journal Debrief   If people on your team keep journals (which is a good idea for anyone who wants to become a better leader or team member), develop two or three questions, and give seven to ten minutes for people to answer the questions in their journals. When time is up, ask whether anyone has an insight he or she would share with the group. Depending on the topic, people may or may not choose to reveal what they've written.

Journal questions work for debriefing when the goal is personal reflection:

- "How would an outsider say you contribute to this situation?"

- "What's one thing you personally can do to improve this situation?"

- "What's one thing you will do differently in our next iteration?"

- "What is one change you can commit to in the next iteration?"

Question Pairs   Pick a pair of questions to encourage team members to talk about the activity. Question pairs might be as follows:

- What interesting things happened during this activity? What did you learn about yourself or your teammates?

- How was your experience in the activity like other things that have happened in the team (or during the iteration)? What team strengths showed up?

- How has your thinking changed after this activity? If you could go back and change only one thing, what would it be?

What If Encourage the team to think in new ways. Ask "what if...?" questions.

- What if the timeline had been ordered from present to past instead of from past to present?

- What if you had twice as much time for brainstorming?

- What if different people had been in the small groups?

- What if we started the activity over right now?

Activities Quick Reference Matrix

Wondering when to use which activities? Here's a quick reference. The table on the next page lists all the activities described in this book by retrospective phase and by the type of retrospective where the activity is useful.

Activities

Phase	Activity	Iteration	Release	End of Project
Set the Stage	ESVP	✓	✓	✓
	Check-in	✓		
	Focus On/Focus Off			
	Working Agreements	✓	✓	✓
Gather Data	Triple Nickels	✓	✓	✓
	Time Line and Variations	✓	✓	✓
	Color-Coded Dots	✓	✓	✓
	Locating Project Strengths	✓	✓	✓
	Identify Themes	✓	✓	✓
	Mad, Sad, Glad	✓	✓	✓
Generate Insights	Patterns and Shifts	✓	✓	✓
	Fishbone	✓	✓	✓
	5 Whys	✓		
	Report Out and Synthesis	✓	✓	✓
	Brainstorming/Filtering	✓	✓	✓
	Force Field Analysis		✓	✓
	Prioritize with Dots	✓	✓	✓
Decide What to Do	The Retrospective Planning Game		✓	✓
	Academy Awards		✓	✓
	Triple Nickels	✓	✓	✓
	SMART Goals	✓	✓	✓
Close the Retrospective	+/Delta	✓		
	Appreciations	✓	✓	✓
	Temperature Reading	✓	✓	✓

Figure 27—Activities by Retrospective Phase and Type of Retrospective

Resources for Learning Facilitation Skills

Three organizations that offer facilitation training:

- Technology of Participation, Group Facilitation Methods Course: http://www.ica-usa.org/top/courses/crsgfm.html

- Community at Work, Group Facilitation Skills: http://www.communityatwork.com/groupfac.html

- The Grove Consultants International for workshops on facilitation and graphic recording: http://www.grove.com

To supplement training, practice, and observation, here are three excellent books:

- *The Facilitator's Guide to Participatory Decision-Making* by Kaner, Lind, Toldi, Fisk, and Berger (New Society Publishers, 1996)

- *The Skilled Facilitator* (revised edition) by Roger Schwartz (Jossey-Bass, 2002)

- *The Art of Focused Conversation: 100 Ways to Access Group Wisdom in the Workplace* edited by R. Brian Stanfield (New Society Publishers, 2000)

Bibliography

[Bri03]   William Bridges. *Managing Transitions: Making the Most of Change*. Da Capo Press, Cambridge, MA, 2003.

[Dav05]   Rachel Davies. Improvising Space for a Timeline. *Email*. personal, 2005.

[Der02]   Esther Derby. Climbing the learning curve: Practice with feedback. *Insights*. [Fall], 2002.

[Der03]   Esther Derby. How to Improve Meetings When You're Not in Charge. *http://www.stickyminds.com*. online, 2003.

[Der03a]   Esther Derby. The Roti Method for Gauging Meeting Effectiveness. *http://www.stickyminds.com*. online, 2003.

[Der05]   Esther Derby. Helping Your Team Weather the Storm. *http://www.stickyminds.com*. online, 2005.

[Hin05]   Siegi Hinger. Re: Improvising Space for a Timeline. *Email*. personal, 2005.

[Kel87]   J. M. Keller. Strategies for Stimulating the Motivation to Learn. *Performance and Instruction*. 26[8]:1–7, 1987.

[Ker01]   Norman L. Kerth. *Project Retrospectives: A Handbook for Team Reviews*. Dorset House, New York, NY, USA, 2001.

[Mac03]   Tim MacKinnon. XP—Call in the Social Workers. *http://www.macta.f2s.com/Thoughts/Papers/XP%20Call%20In%20the%20social*. online, 2003.

[Sat91]   Virginia Satir. *The Satir Model: Family Therapy and Beyond*. Science and Behavior Books, Palo Alto, CA, 1991.

[Sch90]   Johanna Schwab. *A Resource Handbook for Satir Concepts*. Science and Behavior Books, Palo Alto, CA, 1990.

[Sch94]   Roger Schwarz. *The Skilled Facilitator*. Jossey-Bass Publishers, San Francisco, CA, 1994.

[Sta97]   R. Brian Standield. *The Art of Focused Conversation: 100 Ways to Access Group Wisdom in the Workplace*. The Canadian Institute of Cultural Affairs, Toronto, Canada, 1997.

[WM01]   Jane Magruder Watkins and Bernard J. Mohr. *Appreciative Inquiry: Change at the Speed of Imagination*. Jossey-Bass Publishers, San Francisco, CA, 2001.

Index

Be Agile

Don't just "do" agile; you want *be* agile. We'll show you how.

The best agile book isn't a book: *Agile in a Flash* is a unique deck of index cards that fit neatly in your pocket. You can tape them to the wall. Spread them out on your project table. Get stains on them over lunch. These cards are meant to be used, not just read.

Jeff Langr and Tim Ottinger
(110 pages) ISBN: 9781934356715. $15
http://pragprog.com/titles/olag

Here are three simple truths about software development:

1. You can't gather all the requirements up front. 2. The requirements you do gather will change. 3. There is always more to do than time and money will allow.

Those are the facts of life. But you can deal with those facts (and more) by becoming a fierce software-delivery professional, capable of dispatching the most dire of software projects and the toughest delivery schedules with ease and grace.

Jonathan Rasmusson
(280 pages) ISBN: 9781934356586. $34.95
http://pragprog.com/titles/jtrap

Get Results

Reading about new techniques is one thing, making them work in your company and on your team is another matter entirely. Here's the help you need.

If you work with people, you need this book. Learn to read co-workers' and users' *patterns of resistance* and dismantle their objections. With these techniques and strategies you can master the art of evangelizing and help your organization adopt your solutions.

Terrence Ryan
(200 pages) ISBN: 9781934356609. $32.95
http://pragprog.com/titles/trevan

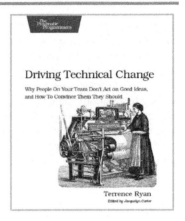

Discover how to coach your team to become more Agile. *Agile Coaching* de-mystifies agile practices—it's a practical guide to creating strong agile teams. Packed with useful tips from practicing agile coaches Rachel Davies and Liz Sedley, this book gives you coaching tools that you can apply whether you are a project manager, a technical lead, or working in a software team.

Rachel Davies and Liz Sedley
(248 pages) ISBN: 9781934356432. $34.95
http://pragprog.com/titles/sdcoach

Think Better

Want to concentrate more effectively, and learn how to take advantage of your brain's wiring? We've got you covered.

Do you ever look at the clock and wonder where the day went? You spent all this time at work and didn't come close to getting everything done. Tomorrow, try something new. Use the Pomodoro Technique, originally developed by Francesco Cirillo, to work in focused sprints throughout the day. In *Pomodoro Technique Illustrated*, Staffan Nöteberg shows you how to organize your work to accomplish more in less time. There's no need for expensive software or fancy planners. You can get started with nothing more than a piece of paper, a pencil, and a kitchen timer.

Staffan Nöteberg
(144 pages) ISBN: 9781934356500. $24.95
http://pragprog.com/titles/snfocus

Software development happens in your head. Not in an editor, IDE, or design tool. You're well educated on how to work with software and hardware, but what about *wetware*—our own brains? Learning new skills and new technology is critical to your career, and it's all in your head.

In this book by Andy Hunt, you'll learn how our brains are wired, and how to take advantage of your brain's architecture. You'll learn new tricks and tips to learn more, faster, and retain more of what you learn.

You need a pragmatic approach to thinking and learning. You need to *Refactor Your Wetware.*

Andy Hunt
(288 pages) ISBN: 9781934356050. $34.95
http://pragprog.com/titles/ahptl

Lead Better

So you're the manager. Whether it's one project or a whole portfolio, learn what you need to do to make it work.

This book is a reality-based guide for modern projects. You'll learn how to recognize your project's potholes and ruts, and determine the best way to fix problems—without causing more problems.

Johanna Rothman
(360 pages) ISBN: 9780978739249. $34.95
http://pragprog.com/titles/jrpm

Too many projects? Want to organize them and evaluate them without getting buried under a mountain of statistics? This book will help you collect all your work, decide which projects you should do first, second—and *never*. You'll see how to tie your work to your organization's mission and show your board, your managers, and your staff what you can accomplish and when. You'll get a better view of the work you have, and learn how to make those difficult decisions, ensuring that all your strength is focused where it needs to be.

Johanna Rothman
(200 pages) ISBN: 9781934356296. $32.95
http://pragprog.com/titles/jrport

The Pragmatic Bookshelf

The Pragmatic Bookshelf features books written by developers for developers. The titles continue the well-known Pragmatic Programmer style and continue to garner awards and rave reviews. As development gets more and more difficult, the Pragmatic Programmers will be there with more titles and products to help you stay on top of your game.

Visit Us Online

This Book's Home Page
http://pragprog.com/titles/dlret
Source code from this book, errata, and other resources. Come give us feedback, too!

Register for Updates
http://pragprog.com/updates
Be notified when updates and new books become available.

Join the Community
http://pragprog.com/community
Read our weblogs, join our online discussions, participate in our mailing list, interact with our wiki, and benefit from the experience of other Pragmatic Programmers.

New and Noteworthy
http://pragprog.com/news
Check out the latest pragmatic developments, new titles and other offerings.

Save on the eBook

Save on the eBook versions of this title. Owning the paper version of this book entitles you to purchase the electronic versions at a terrific discount.

PDFs are great for carrying around on your laptop—they are hyperlinked, have color, and are fully searchable. Most titles are also available for the iPhone and iPod touch, Amazon Kindle, and other popular e-book readers.

Buy now at *http://pragprog.com/coupon*

Contact Us

Online Orders:	*http://pragprog.com/catalog*
Customer Service:	*support@pragprog.com*
International Rights:	*translations@pragprog.com*
Academic Use:	*academic@pragprog.com*
Write for Us:	*http://pragprog.com/write-for-us*
Or Call:	+1 800-699-7764

CPSIA information can be obtained
at www.ICGtesting.com
Printed in the USA
BVOW09s1558150317

478600BV00012B/107/P